Reducing Recidivism

Reducing Recidivism

A Focus on Rehabilitation Instead of Punishment

Cathy Cowling

LEXINGTON BOOKS
Lanham • Boulder • New York • London

Published by Lexington Books
An imprint of The Rowman & Littlefield Publishing Group, Inc.
4501 Forbes Boulevard, Suite 200, Lanham, Maryland 20706
www.rowman.com

86-90 Paul Street, London EC2A 4NE

British Library Cataloguing in Publication Information Available

Library of Congress Cataloging-in-Publication Data

ISBN 9781793626318 (cloth) | ISBN 9781793626325 (ebook)

∞™ The paper used in this publication meets the minimum requirements of American National Standard for Information Sciences—Permanence of Paper for Printed Library Materials, ANSI/NISO Z39.48-1992.

Contents

Foreword

Recidivism remains a critical societal concern. In the United States, as many as 7 out of 10 former inmates are rearrested within 5 years of release (James, 2015, p. 6). Unfortunately, this and other related statistics on recidivism makes the United States' recidivism rate among the highest of all the world's countries (Benecchi, 2021). This is certainly not a badge of distinction that "We the people" should wear with pride!

The economic costs of recidivism are staggering. The costs are the sum total of federal, state, and local expense to maintain the prison system and the lost contribution to the annual GDP. Taxpayers are spending approximately $80 billion to fund the federal, state, and local prison system (Lockwood and Lewis, 2019). Further, it is estimated that recidivism cuts the annual GDP by as much as $65 billion per year (Muresianu, 2018). The total loss to the country's economy is nearly $150 billion annually. Shocking!

While it is unrealistic to think it is possible to eliminate entirely the cost of funding the prison system and to reclaim the revenue of lost productivity, it is possible to curb the cost and the loss. Each ex-offender incarcerated costs the taxpayers on average $37,441 annually (Bureau of Prisons, 2018). Therefore, reducing recidivism has a direct and immediate effect on reducing costs. If the ex-offender is placed successfully in a place of employment, the revenue of lost productivity can also be recovered.

The human costs of recidivism are equally staggering. The tragic truth is many offenders struggle with diverse issues that may for them become impediments to reintegration into life "outside." The array of issues facing the former offender may include economic, health, mental, addiction, or personal hurdles. Some offenders may lack social capital and, therefore, suffer from poor interpersonal skills. Others may have and are returning to dysfunctional marital or familial relationships. Many may return to former nefarious peer groups. Most have little to no higher education and lack the professional or skilled labor credentials to interview for jobs that provide a living wage. Furthermore, the former offender may be continuing to struggle with unresolved issues related to mental or sexual abuse, a poor employment history, isolation, poor decision-making capabilities, and no support network.

If incarceration alone was the answer to rehabilitating an offender, the recidivism rate would be zero. Obviously, imprisonment alone is not the deterrent or remedy to reducing recidivism. So what, then, is the answer? Perhaps the answer is at the intersection of retributive, restorative, and rehabilitative justice. Without doubt, an offender needs to "pay the price" for the crime committed. Certainly, we can create a better society by learning from victims and offenders who genuinely are seeking forgiveness and extending grace. But, most importantly, incarceration must include rehabilitation that address the multiplicity of needs offenders embody.

In her latest book, *Reducing Recidivism,* Cathy Cowling addresses the difficult and complicated challenges of reducing recidivism by tackling the need to make incarceration a comprehensive and inclusive rehabilitative process, in addition to retributive. In addition to presenting the statistical data demonstrating the problems and the associated societal concerns, she lists for consideration specific areas of acute need that have proven results in reducing recidivism.

- Education
- Employment training
- Treatments and programs that address specific health, addiction, and mental/behavioral/cognitive issues
- Comprehensive reentry programs
- Faith and family
- Social capital

Dr. Cowling is correct. Recidivism is a difficult problem that needs to be addressed both inside and outside of the criminal justice system. It is my earnest prayer that this book can spark such conversation.

John Roberson
Buies Creek
November 29, 2021

Acknowledgments

I wish to thank the many people who contributed to the completion of this book. I must first thank the Bob Barker Foundation for the idea of researching the effects of education on recidivism. Dr. John Roberson greatly supported my efforts and is a true believer in rehabilitation. Dr. James Martin has been my teacher, mentor, and example throughout my adult life, and I hope to make him proud. The Campbell students at Sampson Correctional were inspirational and lent reality to the theories I had studied. Kelli Vann has provided critical administrative support. I have also been blessed with several wonderful research assistants: Matthew Cappello, Casidy Havird, and Kaitlyn Lancaster. Thank you so much. Finally, I wish to thank my daughter, Beth. The desire to do well for her sake gave me the push I needed to keep going.

Introduction

Many Americans fear crime and do not wish to assist those convicted of crimes. They do not support funding for rehabilitation or education programs for prisoners. They wish to keep criminals away from society. However, a large percentage (up to 95%) of those sent to prison will at some point be released (Hughes and Wilson, 2004). Many formerly incarcerated people commit new crimes and are returned to prison, at great cost to Americans. Perhaps Americans agree with the Martinson (1974) report that "nothing works" to rehabilitate offenders. It seems illogical to expect a different outcome after prison without some sort of intervention or treatment. Before advocating for a means of solving the crime and recidivism problem, there are two basic questions that need to be answered. First, can people be changed? Secondly, if people can be changed, what is the proper role of prison in achieving this change?

An individual's answer to the first question, "Can people be changed?," often depends on a person's background and religious affiliation. However, criminal punishment has historically been linked with reformation and rehabilitation. In fact, our system of punishment is called corrections. It is designed to correct mistakes in behavior. This book will assume that people can be changed. This does not mean that every attempt at rehabilitation or reformation will be successful, but rehabilitation programs can decrease the return to crime.

The second question is one of penal philosophy, which leads to the question, "What is the purpose of prison?" If people can be changed, then what steps should the system take to create change? One philosophy of corrections is retribution. This means that the goal is punishment and revenge. The offender should suffer an amount of pain equal to the pain that the victim suffered. Punishment should hurt enough to satisfy the need for justice. This is the prevalent philosophy of punishment in the United States (Sumrall, Sumrall, and Doss, 2016).

Similarly, the goal of incapacitation states that the purpose of prison should be to physically restrain dangerous offenders from being able to harm others by keeping them incarcerated. Specifically, very dangerous and violent offenders should be isolated to keep the public safe (Sumrall, Sumrall, and Doss, 2016).

Deterrence philosophy argues that the punishment of prison should be harsh enough that the defendant (or others who witness the punishment) will not wish to repeat the crime. This is tough to support, given that a majority of those released from prison return. The problem with both deterrence and incapacitation is that once the measures of deterrence and incapacitation are removed, there no reason for the offender to stop offending (Sumrall, Sumrall, and Doss, 2016).

Rehabilitation suggests that the purpose of sanctions is to lead the offender from a law-breaking path to a law-abiding one. The process of rehabilitation involves education, substance abuse treatment, and other programming that changes the offender's desire to offend. It assumes that offenders can change and that prison programs can help. Once rehabilitated, the offender will not wish to offend any longer (Sumrall, Sumrall, and Doss, 2016). They will no longer need to be incapacitated or deterred. That is the overall premise of this book. This vicious cycle can be stopped and both former offenders and society will benefit.

WHAT IS RECIDIVISM?

One of America's most serious problems, and certainly the most pressing problem for the criminal justice system, is the number of people in prison in the United States. It is a drain on economic resources and a blight on communities. Many of the people in prison have returned to prison for a subsequent sentence, otherwise known as recidivism. This is most simply defined as the return to prison by an individual who has already served time for a prior crime. To understand recidivism further, aspects such as programs and solutions created to reduce recidivism and the effects of these programs must be explored and promoted. Programs that assist will be highlighted throughout this book in hopes that such programs will proliferate.

DEFINITION OF RECIDIVISM

According to the National Institute of Justice, recidivism "refers to a person's relapse into criminal behavior, often after the person receives sanctions or undergoes intervention for a previous crime. Recidivism is measured by criminal acts that result in rearrest, reconviction, or return to prison with or without a new sentence during a three-year period following the prisoner's release" (National Institute of Justice, 2014, p. 1). Return to prison is the most common measurement of recidivism. As the prisons in America are very overcrowded, it is critical to shut this revolving door.

Recidivism is typically measured at one year, two years, three years, and five years after release. It can be measured in three ways: as rearrest for a new crime, conviction for a new crime, or incarceration for a new crime. Rearrest "classifies a person as a recidivist if he or she has been arrested for a new crime after being released into the community directly on probation or after serving a term of imprisonment" (Crime in America, 2021). Reconviction classifies a person as a recidivist if an arrest resulted in a subsequent court conviction. Reincarceration "classifies a person as a recidivist if a conviction or revocation resulted in a prison or jail sentence as punishment." The reincarceration measure counts offenders who were reported returned to the Federal Bureau of Prisons, state prison, or local jail for any term of incarceration (Dumville and Hunt, 2016).

HOW MANY PRISONERS RECIDIVATE?

In 2015, 580,900 state and 60,200 federal prisoners were released from prisons in the United States (Bureau of Prisons, Justice, 2016). What many people just don't realize is how many of them return to prison. According to the National Institute of Justice, 35% of prisoners return to prison within two years of release, 67.8% return to prison within three years of release, and 76.6% return to prison within five years of release (National Institute of Justice, 2014).

In 2002, 41% of jail inmates had a current or prior violent offense; 46% were nonviolent recidivists; and 13% had a current or prior drug offense (James, 2004). Almost three-quarters (72.8%) of federal offenders sentenced in fiscal year 2016 had been convicted of a prior offense. The average number of previous convictions was 6.1 among offenders with a criminal history (Dumville and Hunt, 2016). Clearly, many do not seem to mind returning. A burning question in the minds of many Americans is why they return. Some citizens question whether conditions are harsh enough.

According to another study, 43% of offenders released were rearrested during an eight-year period. Among the offenders, 31.7% were convicted of a new crime, and one-quarter of the offenders went back to prison within eight years. Most offenders who recidivated were rearrested within the first two years. The average time between release and rearrest was twenty-one months. Among federal offenders, those with a more serious criminal record were more likely to recidivate. Age was also a factor in predicting recidivism. Those who were released when younger than twenty-one had the highest rate of recidivism (67.6%). Offenders who were older than sixty years when released had the lowest rate of recidivism (16.0%) (Dumville and Hunt, 2016).

Other factors, including offense type and educational level, were associated with differing rates of recidivism. Education level is also a good predictor of recidivism rates. Those who were released and did not hold a high school diploma had the highest recidivism rates (60.4%). Those offenders with a high school diploma recidivated at a rate of 50.7%, and those with some college recidivated at a rate of 39.3%. College graduates had the lowest rate of recidivism at 19.1% (Dumville and Hunt, 2016).

The type of offense committed was also related to the rate of recidivism. Those with a prior firearms offense were most likely to recidivate (68.3%). Those with a prior robbery offense recidivated at a rate of 67.3%, while 55.7% of those with immigration offenses reoffended. 49.9% of those with a history of drug trafficking recidivated, and 44.45% of those convicted of larceny recidivated. 32.4% of those with a fraud conviction recidivated (Dumville and Hunt, 2016).

WHY SHOULD THE GENERAL PUBLIC CARE?

There are many reasons why the American public should be concerned about the incredibly high rate of recidivism. These reasons include the contribution of recidivism to America's mass incarceration, costs of future crime, and costs of future incarceration. These issues particularly affect minority communities.

MASS INCARCERATION

In October 2013, the incarceration rate in the United States of America was the highest in the world, at 716 inmates per 100,000 people in the national population. This rate exceeds even nations with poor human rights records like Russia, China, and Saudi Arabia. While the United States represents only 4.4% of the world's population, it houses 22% of the world's prisoners. The United States has been called "the world leader in incarcerations," a dubious distinction. More than two million people are currently incarcerated in the United States. This represents a 500% increase in prisoners over the last forty years. Due to the "war on drugs" and a movement to get tough on crime, more people are initially receiving prison sentences, and prison sentences are also getting longer (The Sentencing Project, 2020). The tough on crime approach includes policies that favor harsher sentences for recidivists and fewer opportunities for rehabilitation. Lack of public support for rehabilitation also contributes.

In a further study, the Bureau of Justice Statistics (BJS) reported that for the first time in years, Texas took the lead reporting the highest number of imprisoned citizens. With this in mind, Texas "now has the nation's largest incarcerated population under the jurisdiction of the prison system" (Justice Policy Institute, 2000). On a larger, national, scale, "one in five new prisoners added to the nation's prisons (18%) was in Texas (Texas Tough, 2000). According to the 2022 prison population by state, Texas is still ahead of California with regard to the largest incarcerated population with Texas' total prison population being 154,479 and California's being 122,417 (World Population Review, 2023). Since 1983, Texas' incarceration trends have increased an astounding 328%, with Kenedy County having the highest overall admission rates (Henrichson et al, 2019). Overall, while California has a larger overall population, its imprisonment rate is much lower than that of Texas, which has allowed Texas to claim a higher imprisonment rate, as shown in recent studies.

Mass incarceration and get-tough policies are part of a correctional philosophy in the United States that has been based on retribution rather than rehabilitation. Retribution, sentencing based on punishment, has been the lead correctional philosophy in the United States for many years. Americans and their law makers are not willing to invest in rehabilitation programs and are instead simply warehousing those sentenced to incarceration.

The impact of mass incarceration is not equal, however. Minorities make up 37% of the US population but 67% of the prison population (Prison Policy Initiative, n.d.) US incarceration rates by race and ethnicity in 2010: 450/100k whites incarcerated, 831/100k Latinos incarcerated, 2,306/100k blacks incarcerated (Prison Policy Initiative, n.d.). This creates problems for minority communities both socially and economically. When people are incarcerated, they may come out unprepared to reenter society.

FUTURE CRIME

An obvious reason to work to reduce recidivism is the damage and harm caused by repeated offenses to the public. Those who commit future crimes not only return to prison but harm others in society. The costs of future crime include actual crime costs and incarceration costs. In 2014, over one million violent crimes, including aggravated assault, robbery, rape, and murder were reported to police (Federal Bureau of Investigation, 2015).

In 2012, the direct costs of violent crime in America in terms of police, courts, and corrections reached $460 billion. That averages $3257 per taxpayer (D'Abruzzo and Chapman, 2016). Also, during 2014, more than eight million property crimes were reported, costing victims $14.3 million in direct financial losses. Many these crimes were committed by those who have already been convicted of a crime and committed another crime after being released from prison. By reducing the rate of recidivism, the number of crimes committed, and the financial and physical damage associated with those crimes to people and their property could be reduced.

PRISON COSTS

In addition to the harm to people and their property, the return to prison comes at a great financial cost to American taxpayers. The average cost to house a prisoner in 2015 was $31,977 or $87.61 per day (Bureau of Prisons, Justice, 2016). Overall, in 2015, Americans spent between $39 billion and $45 billion to house state and federal prisoners (Bureau of Prisons, Justice, 2016). Two states dealing with an exceptionally high cost of keeping offenders in prison are New York and California. According to the *New York Times*, it costs $167,731 to house each inmate in New York City jails in 2012. New York state paid $60,000 per inmate in state prisons during the same year (Santora, 2013).

California represents at 20% of the nation's total prison spending and has the largest state prison system. Their prison population is around 132,000 (D'Abruzzo and Chapman, 2016). California's corrections budget for 2017 was $11.4 billion. This averages to a per inmate cost of $75,560, which, the *Los Angeles Times* points out, is more than tuition at Harvard (Associated Press, 2017).

A more average example is North Carolina. The state spent just over $1.3 billion in 2017 to house prisoners. This is based on an average cost per inmate of $35,252 and a prison population of about 37,000 (North Carolina Department of Public Safety, 2019).

OBSTACLES THAT LEAD TO RECIDIVISM

While the cost of recidivism is great, there are many reasons why an offender may choose to recidivate or may feel they have no chance but to recidivate. These include individual and neighborhood characteristics and being around others who reoffend. Other factors that specifically contributed to recidivism are male gender, drug involvement, and living in areas with high rates of recidivism. Those who were older when released and who had been convicted of violent and drug offenses were less likely to recidivate (Stahler et al.,

2013). Furthermore, "released prisoners typically face obstacles in obtaining employment and stable housing often due to lack of work skills, stigma, and low levels of educational attainment" (Petersilia, 2003).

Barriers to successful reentry include employment, education, housing, voting rights, and health care (Lattimore and Visher, 2014). According to the Center for Justice and Reconciliation, the keys to prepare prisoners for reentry are: finding mentors, reuniting families, developing communities, planning ahead, locating resources, avoiding trouble, making amends, and serving others (Global Justice Resource Center, n.d.).

Many of those reentering society also experience difficulties of returning to a problematic family and social environment, chronic health problems, unresolved substance abuse, mental health problems, and numerous other challenges in establishing a conventional prosocial lifestyle (Mallik-Kane and Visher, 2008; National Research Council, 2007; Petersilia, 2003; Visher and Travis, 2003). A typical situation for released offenders is arriving home "with very little money, resources, or social capital, and because of their felony record they are unable to obtain employment or find housing" (Makarios, Steiner, and Travis, 2010, p. 1377). Petersilia (2003) argues that because of these deficits, successful reentry for many prison inmates is both difficult and unlikely. Without changing many of these factors, successful law-abiding behavior is difficult, and recidivism will occur.

Recently incarcerated individuals had an especially hard time accessing needed resources in rural communities. In these areas, there are fewer employment options, fewer housing options, and fewer programs and community resources for mental health and substance abuse. Rural resources are also often far apart with limited public transportation options, and availability and quality vary a great deal.

What works for successful reentry is constantly being evaluated, and evidence-based practice is absolutely necessary. Lattimore and Visher (2014) suggest a new approach. "Many reentry specialists are encouraging a broader focus on comprehensive reentry strategies, not specific programs" (p. 2). Strategies can include many different government agencies, coordination between different agencies, and even inclusion of agencies that are not typically part of the justice system or reentry programs. These strategies can increase success in employment, substance abuse, and general health in addition to traditional recidivism measures. Successful programs address specific risk issues and specific needs, such a mental health, substance abuse, and employment, and assist with a wide range of needs by using targeted individualized approaches. Using different modes of instruction that match with the offenders' learning styles also increases effectiveness of the program. The ultimate goal is a seamless transition between the prison and the community (Lattimore and Visher, 2014).

REDUCTION OF RECIDIVISM IN RECENT YEARS AND THE SECOND ACT GRANT PROGRAM

The good news is that recidivism rates have been going down in recent years. There are several initiatives that have been designed to reduce the return to prison. One of these programs that has been highly effective is the Second Chance Act Pell Grant Program. The grants are administered by US Department of Justice's Office of Justice Programs. The program grants financial support to state and local governments as well as nonprofit organizations in forty-nine states in order to reduce recidivism. Many types of programs are funded through these grants, which include substance abuse and mental health treatment, community-based transition and reentry services, supervision innovations, technology-based career training, and juvenile reentry programs. More than 800 grants have been made since the program began in 2009. In the states discussed below, Second Chance Act grants were coupled with state legislation aimed at reducing recidivism (Council of State Governments Justice Center, 2020).

Using Second Chance Act grants, Colorado has seen its rate of parole revocations fall 25% from a rate of 39% revocations to a rate of 30% revocations between 2008 and 2015. There was a 24% drop in the three-year measure of reincarceration between 2006 and 2012: a decrease from 18% to 14%. Colorado also saw an overall drop in violent crime of 19% between 2006 and 2015. Colorado was awarded seventeen Second Chance Act grants totaling $9.5 million. Four of the grants were used to expand screening, assessment, and treatment for mental health and substance abuse issues. Two grants were used to implement evidence-based supervision strategies in state agencies. In addition, in 2010, Colorado initiated reforms including reduced penalties for low-level drug offenses, parole board consideration of mental health and substance abuse before revocation of parole, and incentives for those on probation to remain compliant including early termination of supervision (Council of State Government Justice Center, 2020).

In similar fashion, Georgia experienced a 35% decline in parole revocations between 2007 and 2016. The state saw a 21% drop in the violent crime rate from 2006 to 2015. Georgia was the recipient of twenty-four Second Chance Act awards totaling $14.5 million. There were statewide recidivism reduction grants to help policymakers and correctional departments plan and implement reforms to reduce recidivism. Four of the grants were used to assist state and local agencies to implement projects that address key challenges faced by those released back to their communities, focusing on those at medium to high risk of reoffending. Georgia's House Bill 1176, passed in 2012, prioritized prison beds for people who commit violent offenses;

strengthened probation, drug courts, and other sentencing alternatives for those who commit nonviolent offenses through expansion of evidence-based practices and additional funding for behavioral health; and expanded Department of Corrections processes to track and measure employment, substance use issues, and payment of victim restitution.

Also using Second Chance Grants, Michigan experienced a 43% decline in people returning to prison from parole between 2006 and 2015. The state's total prison population declined from 16,018 to 13,472. There was a 20% drop in rearrests rate for those on parole, a 20% decline in the three-year reincarceration rate, and a 26% decline in the violent crime rate in Michigan between 2003 and 2012. Michigan was given fourteen Second Chance awards worth $7.4 million. One grant was used for the Department of Corrections to establish career-training programs in prison-technology based jobs and connect participants to employment opportunities post-release. Another grant enabled one county to expand substance use treatment and parenting programs for those who are incarcerated. The state's 2005 Prisoner Reentry Initiative included a transition accountability plan to assess one's risks, needs, and strengths to identify ways to reduce risk, address needs, build upon strengths for success, integrate an interdisciplinary approach to reentry across health care, behavioral health, employment, education, and family support, and create partnerships across probation and parole to improve continuity of services after release.

Using Second Chance funding, North Carolina saw a 42% reduction in probation revocations between 2006 and 2015. There was, in addition, a 46% decrease in the probation revocation rate, from 34% in 2006 to 18% in 2015. North Carolina had a 7% decrease in the two-year reincarceration rate and a 26% drop in violent crime during that same time. North Carolina used nine Second Chance Act grants totaling $3.6 million. Two of the awards allowed local jurisdictions to expand screening, assessment, and pre- and post-release treatment for mental health and substance abuse offenders. Two grants funded pilot projects addressing challenges faced upon release that led to recidivism. One grant enabled state agencies to develop more effective supervision practices that address the needs of the offenders with serious and persistent mental health concerns. The state's Juvenile Reinvestment Act of 2011 invested resources in substance abuse treatment, cognitive behavioral programs, and other evidence-based programming. It also empowered probation officers to use swift and certain jail sanctions in lieu of full revocation and required mandatory supervision for those convicted of felonies to help reduce recidivism.

North Carolina's southern neighbor, South Carolina, boasted a 46% drop in technical revocations between 2010 and 2015. It also experienced a 21% drop in the three year reincarceration rate between 2004 and 2013, a 25% drop in the reincarceration rate for people on supervision from 2010 to 2012, and a

16% drop in the violent crime rate between 2010 and 2015. South Carolina claimed two Second Chance Grants adding up to $800,000. One grant was spent for a nonprofit organization to provide pre- and post-release mentoring and transitional services. The second grant permitted the Department of Probation, Parole, Pardon Services to test new approaches to improve outcomes for those under supervision and to use evidence-based strategies. South Carolina's Crime Reeducation and Sentencing Reform Act of 2010 mandated post-release supervision, authorized earned discharge, enhanced available administrative responses to supervision violations, and restructured penalties for certain violent, property, and drug offenses, all of which was to reserve prison space for more serious offenders.

Finally, Texas experienced a 33% decline in revocations resulting in prison sentences for people on parole between 2007 and 2016. The state saw a 25% drop in the three-year reincarceration rate from 2004 to 2013, a 6% decline in rearrest rates from 2004 to 2013, and a 20% drop in the violent crime rate from 2006 to 2015. Texas was awarded thirty-five Second Chance Grant awards worth a total of $16 million. Two of the grants went for nonprofit organizations to support young parents with mentoring, transitional reentry, parenting skills development, and family engagement. Two grants benefitted a court and a county and allowed them to collaborate with corrections agencies to provide reentry services to people whose geographic area has a disproportionate number of people being released from prison. Three of the grants allowed local agencies to establish or enhance programs that provide family-based substance use treatment for those incarcerated. Texas' Justice Reinvestment Policy Framework, which became law in 2007, enhanced the use of parole for people at low risk of reoffending, expanded more treatment and diversion programs, incentivized counties to create progressive sanctioning models for those on probation, and expanded capacity of substance use treatment programs and intermediate sanction facilities to divert people from prison (National Reentry Resource Center, 2017). Table I.1 lays put these grants.

SECOND CHANCE ACT GRANT PROGRAMS BY STATE

The First Step Act was established on May 22, 2018, and passed by the US House of Representatives. Its initiative allocated $50 million each year, for five years, for prison programming reducing recidivism. Further, it provides specific benefits to federal prisoners including sentence reductions, free telephone, and videoconferencing privileges. The First Step Act's programs include social learning and communication, interpersonal skills, anti-bullying, rejection response, and other life skills. For female, pregnant

Table I.1

Colorado	49.5 million in grant money	Significant decline in parole revocations (25%), reincarceration rates (24%), and an overall drop in violent crime (19%). Grants resulting in supervision strategies, expansion of screening, assessment, and treatment for mental health and substance abuse, as well as parole board consideration.
Georgia	$14.5 million in grant money between twenty-four grants	Significant decline in parole revocations (35%) and overall drop in violent crime (21%). Grants focused on reduction of recidivism causes and rates.
Michigan	$7.4 million in grant money	Recidivism rate decrease (43%), reduction in parole rearrests (20%), decline in three-year reincarceration rate (20%), and decline in overall violent crime (26%). Establishment of career training programs, substance use treatment, parenting programs, etc.
North Carolina	$3.6 million in grant money.	Reduction in probation revocations (42%), decrease in two-year reincarceration rate (7%), overall drop in violent crime (26%). Expansion of screening and assessment for pre- and post- release mental health and substance abuse treatment. Further exploration of recidivism challenges. Juvenile Reinvestment Act for juvenile recidivism concerns.
South Carolina	$800,000 in grant money	Significant decrease in technical revocations (46%), three-year reincarceration rate (21%), and overall drop in violent crime rate (16%). Grants spent for pre and post release mentoring and transitional services. Also allowed probation and parole services to assess new approaches.

Texas	$16 million in grant money	Significant decline in revocations (33%), three-year reincarceration rates (25%), rearrest rates (6%), and drop in overall violent crime rates (20%). Support for young parents with mentoring and transition skills. Provided reentry services as well as established family-based substance abuse treatment.

inmates, it prohibits the use of restraints. In addition, for inmates it ensures they are incarcerated no more than 500 miles from family or their primary residence. The First Step Act also provides secure firearms storage for the Bureau of Prisons. Overall, however, participation eligibility of the program is based on the crime committed by the offender.

BUREAU OF PRISONS EVIDENCE-BASED REFORMS

In 2015, the Federal Bureau of Prisons announced sweeping evidence-based reforms to reduce recidivism among their inmates. This begins with identifying the inmates' criminogenic risks and need factors that are associated with criminal behavior. In addition, the Bureau is building a school district within their system, including tablet-based, blended courses and use of Second Chance Pell grants. Inmates are encouraged to work in Federal Prison Industries and develop skills for employment after release. Recidivism is being researched, and research is being implemented in evidence-based ways. Mental health is being made a priority. Inmates are assisted in maintaining family ties including giving priority to the special needs of female inmates. Solitary confinement and private prisons are being reduced, and halfway houses are being reformed. Finally, inmates receive aid for getting government identification and reentry resources before their release (Bureau of Prisons, Justice, 2016).

CONGRESSIONAL PUSH TO REDUCE RECIDIVISM

The need to address the problem of recidivism has recently received attention from the US Congress. On May 22, 2018, the US House of Representatives passed the First Step Act. The bill was sponsored by Republican Congressman Doug Collins of Georgia and Democratic Congressman Hakeem Jeffries from New York in a bipartisan effort to reduce recidivism. The bill allocated $50 million each year for five years for prison programming aimed at reducing recidivism (Uria, 2018).

The first part of the legislation provides specific benefits to federal prisoners who take part in evidence-based recidivism reduction programs. Participants can earn good time toward sentence reductions as well as free telephone and videoconferencing privileges up to thirty minutes per day, or 510 minutes per month for completing qualifying programs (Center for Immigration Studies, 2018).

The programs themselves include social learning and communication, interpersonal skills, anti-bullying, rejection response, and other life skills; family relationship building; structured parent-child interaction and parenting skills; classes on morals or ethics; academic classes; cognitive behavioral treatment; mentoring; vocational training; faith-based classes or services; civic engagement and reintegrative community services; and prison jobs (Center for Immigration Studies, 2018).

The second part of the legislation creates secure firearms storage for the Bureau of Prisons. This third portion prohibits the use of restraints (shackles) on pregnant inmates. The fourth portion specifies that federal prisoners cannot be incarcerated more than 500 miles from their family/primary residence and that the Bureau of Prisons shall place prisoners of low risk and lower needs on home confinement for the maximum amount of time permitted (Center for Immigration Studies, 2018).

Some prisoners cannot participate in the program on the basis of their crimes, including those convicted of peonage (debt servitude/slavery/human trafficking). Inmates also cannot participate if they have three misdemeanor convictions, drug crimes, crimes of violence, or aggravated felonies (Center for Immigration Studies, 2018).

THE BOB BARKER FOUNDATION

One leader in in the movement to reduce recidivism is the Bob Barker Foundation, located in Fuquay-Varina, North Carolina. The Bob Barker Corporation is the world's largest distributer of correctional supplies. The corporation established the Bob Barker Foundation, the only nonprofit foundation in America entirely dedicated to reducing recidivism. Each year, 10% of Barker Corporation profits go to the Barker Foundation. The mission of the foundation is "to develop and support programs that help incarcerated individuals successfully reenter society and stay out for life." A $5 million endowment has been set aside to enable funding of these programs. The foundation has awarded more than $2 million to community partners working with those who have recently been released in order to prevent a return to crime. The grants given by the foundation have served more than one million individuals reentering society. The recidivism rate for those working with Barker partners is 12.2% (The Bob Barker Foundation, n.d.).

Among those agencies collaborating with the Barker Foundation are Step Up Ministries, Reaching Out from Within, Project Reentry, Haven House, Christian Library International, and Bridges to Life. Step Up Ministries, located in Raleigh, Durham, and Greensboro, North Carolina is designed to help people to find steady employment. The agency's focus is on reducing the vulnerable situations created for families by unemployment (StepUp Ministry, n.d.).

Reaching Out from Within serves both Kansas and North Carolina. The program focuses on issues of violence and abuse in order to help inmates to stop the cycle of violence. Those in the program examine who they are, and what shaped them, and who they want to become (Reaching Out from Within, n.d.).

Project Re-entry assists offenders and former offenders in their transition to society in thirteen counties in North Carolina. Project Re-entry has served 2,962 offenders with pre-release programs, 869 offenders with pre- to-post release programming, and 2,913 with post-release-only programs (Project Re-entry, n.d.). The mission of Project Re-entry is to "establish a coordinated system of pre- and post-release services between; the North Carolina Department of Public Safety, community resource agencies, the One Stop systems, faith-based initiatives, employers, community residents, and former offenders, to reduce criminal justice costs, improve the reintegration of former offenders and increase public safety." The key components of Project Reentry include pre-release programming, pre- to-post release programming, post-only programming, and community and employer outreach (Project Reentry, n.d.).

Based in Raleigh, North Carolina, Haven House focuses its programming on youth offenders and at-risk youth. The program utilizes programming, advocacy, and community mobilization (Haven House Services, n.d.). Christian Library International is based in North Carolina. It distributes Bibles and Christian literature in prison inmates. Their mission is to develop Christian disciples within prisons in order to promote a better life for former prisoners once they are released (Christian Library International, n.d.).

Bridges to Life operates in Texas and is based on a restorative justice model. Offenders hear the stories of victims in order to experience the concepts of responsibility, accountability, and restitution. Bonds are created between offenders and their families and communities to promote safer communities and reduce recidivism (Bridges to Life, n.d.).

Several initiatives can improve recidivism rates in the United States. While some offenders will not change their behaviors, many can be helped.

Specifically: employment programs, education opportunities, substance abuse treatment, reentry programs, and faith-based programs can significantly reduce recidivism. Moreover, everyone in society can benefit from these initiatives and should be interested in seeing them succeed (Core Civic, 2018). "Research on criminogenic risks and need shows that successful rehabilitative programs tend to include the four indirect factors of employment, education, addiction management, and prosocial activities including family involvement. These four factors contribute to the central eight criminogenic risk factors of criminal history, antisocial personality, attitudes and cognitions," (Sells et al., 2020; Gill and Wilson, 2016). Throughout this book, the ability of these factors to improve success of reentry will be examined.

Chapter 1

Education and Its Effects on Recidivism

One of the best ways to reduce recidivism rates is to provide educational opportunities to those in prison. Research does show a direct link between education of inmates and reduced recidivism. Those who participate in education while in prison have 43% lower odds of recidivating than inmates who did not participate. This means, in effect, reducing the risk of recidivating by 43% for those who participate in correctional education programs versus those who do not. GED programs, adult basic education programs, college programs, and vocational education programs all contribute to reducing recidivism rates. Correctional education in prison also increases the odds of employment after release by 13%. Participation in vocational training while in prison further increases the odds of employment after release by 28% (Davis et al., 2013).

These are not the only gains from prison educational programming. Research suggests that there are five major benefits from prison education. These are personal wellbeing of the inmate, increased human capital (motivation to change, moving forward), social capital (belonging and community, active engagement), knowledge, skills, employability, and a change in prison culture. Prison education is a short-term investment that has long term benefits: development of whole person, prison culture that promotes rehab, participation in society, positive contribution, and sustained employment.

COST EFFECTIVENESS

While educating those who are incarcerated involves an initial investment to provide programs, ultimately that investment pays off. In the end analysis, education is a very cost-effective measure because it reduces the future incarceration costs associated with recidivism. The three-year projected reincarceration costs for a hypothetical pool of one hundred released prisoners who did not receive correctional education is estimated to be between $2.94 million and $3.25 million. The estimated cost for a group of the same size who received education while serving their sentence is between $2.07 million and $2.28 million. Therefore, providing education reduces future costs for this group by $.87 to $.97 million. For a cost of $140,000 to $174,000 to provide correctional education to that pool of 100 ($1400–$1744 per inmate), there is a reduction in future costs between $870,000 and $970,000 (Davis, et. al., 2013). Prison education makes good financial sense.

IMPROVED PRISON CLIMATE AND DISCIPLINE

Attending college classes has further been associated with improving social climate and communications in prison populations and reduced disciplinary infractions. Prison education enrollment provides incentives for good behavior, produces more "responsible, mature individuals who have a calming influence on other prisoners and on prison officers." According to one recipient of prison education, "Education has made me more well-behaved . . . it's had a calming effect . . . gave me something else to think about . . . stopped me acting so impulsively . . . gave me some long-term thoughts" (Farley and Pike, 2016, p. 66–67).

In a survey of inmates in the United Kingdom, 81% of respondents claimed that they participated in education to occupy their time and relieve monotony, 69% said that their education was a way to cope with the stress of incarceration, and 40% said that prison education helped them a lot. Higher education may even make inmates more risk averse. Inmates who received education had increased cognitive ability and new pro-social thinking patterns, and increased communication and negotiation skills that enable them to solve problems without violence. Education in prison leads to improvements in cognitive processing, communication abilities, prosocial behaviors, emotional maturity, empathy, and self-control (Farley and Pike, 2016, p. 66–67).

Students also benefit from their relationships with teachers and tutors, which are based on respect, caring, and positive expectations. These benefits assist with the Risk-Needs-Responsivity rehabilitation model. Overall, prisoners benefit from positive role models like educators (Farley and Pike, 2016, p. 66–67). These models give prisoners something to aspire to.

The most common report across all stakeholder groups at all facilities was that involvement in prison education affects inmate behavior and creates a safer prison environment. Prison educational program students recognized the privilege of being enrolled in these courses and reported being careful to avoid situations that could result in disciplinary infractions and subsequently jeopardize their continued participation (Winterfield et al., 2009).

There are challenges to the success of educating inmates. Prison officials, such as correctional officers, and their attitudes toward prisoners and prison education affect the success of participants in these programs. "Prison officers have the capacity to enhance or undermine the goals of the prison where they work and to either motivate or de-motivate prisoners." (Farley and Pike, 2016). Additionally, continuous participation is necessary for success. However, the needs of the prison such as budgeting and overcrowding may mean ending of programs and transferring of students. This results in many participants not being able to complete educational programs. Finally, prisoners who engage in an educational program are often the first in their family to participate in post-secondary education. For these students, there is lack of support from families and communities.

The goal is not to generate "worker bees" but to enable "incarcerated people to channel their often-prodigious street smarts into more sophisticated forms of inquiry and analysis." Unfortunately, college enrollment behind bars is lower than GED and vocational programs. Only 11% of eligible prison population participated in post-secondary correctional education in 2003–2004. It is easy to get enthusiastic about the "corrections system" as a workshop to fix social undesirables, but many people never belonged anywhere near this broken system to begin with. Delivering long-denied educational opportunities behind bars is not a process of "correcting" the flawed people inside but of correcting injustice that surrounds communities on the outside. Extending Pell Grant access in prisons would mean that students could apply for up to $5,775 for tuition and related expenses at college-level programs offered in prison facilities (Wexler, 2016).

Under the Obama Administration, the Department of Education chose 67 colleges and universities for a Pell Grant pilot program. Second Chance Pell Grants would enroll 12,000 prisoners at more than 100 correctional institutions. The program is geared for those likely to be released within the next five years. Investing in education in prisons saves money and will enable us to measure those savings and benefits by applying this approach.

EXAMPLES OF GOOD EDUCATION PROGRAMS

One of the best examples of programs providing higher education in prison settings is the Hudson Link program in New York State. The program was begun in 1998 and awards about twenty-eight degrees each year through eight colleges in six correctional facilities. The group was begun by inmates, former inmates, community leaders and volunteers. Graduates of the Hudson

Link program have a 4% recidivism rate, compared to a national recidivism rate of 67% (Hudson Link for Higher Education, 2022).

Nine colleges are a part of the Hudson Link consortium: Columbia University, Columbia-Green Community College, Mercy College, Nyack College, Siena College, St. Thomas Aquinas Colleges, SUNY Sullivan, Ulster Community College, and Vassar College. Hudson Link offers associate's and bachelor's degrees in Behavioral Science, Liberal Arts, and Organizational Management. To enter the program, students must have a high school diploma or GED and pass a college placement exam. More than 575 students are currently enrolled (Hudson Link for Higher Education, 2022).

Hudson Link's College Completion Program enables students who have been released before completing their four-year degrees to finish their degree at Nyack College. Students can attend classes on campus and their credits earned in prison will transfer to Nyack for credit. Alumni services provide assistance with job readiness including resume writing, job search, interview attire, laptops and computer training, professional mentoring, and internship opportunities (Hudson Link for Higher Education, 2022).

Various programs are offered at the facilities served by Hudson Link. At Greene Correctional Facility, where half the population is under 21, vocational programs in masonry, electrical, and horticulture as well as Adult Basic Education and GED programs are offered. In addition, Greene Correctional offers a highly competitive college and precollege program (Hudson Link for Higher Education, 2022).

Fishkill Correctional houses 1,800 inmates and, through Hudson Link, offers GED, ESL classes, and a Commercial Arts Program. A bachelor's degree in Agricultural Management and a manufacturing program where inmates make beds, chairs, and computer furniture are also offered at Fishkill. In addition, Fishkill has a creative Puppies Behind Bars program where students train dogs to become service dogs (Hudson Link for Higher Education, 2022).

At Shawangunk Correctional maximum-security prison, inmates can obtain an associate's degree through SUNY Ulster. Students can also get occupational training in building maintenance, carpentry, electrical work, and plumbing (Hudson Link for Higher Education, 2022).

Inmates at Sing Sing correctional facility who do not have a high school degree must enroll in GED classes. Hudson Link offers both associate's and bachelor's degrees in behavioral science. Moreover, New York Theological Seminary provides a master's degree in professional studies. Each year, 1,000 volunteers assist with educational, musical, and religious programs (Hudson Link for Higher Education, 2022).

Through Hudson Link, Sullivan Correctional Facility offers programs for inmates with special needs and has a special unit so that inmates with visual and hearing impairments can participate in classes. Sullivan also offers an associate degree in Liberal Arts (Hudson Link for Higher Education, 2022).

At Taconic Correctional Facility for women, Hudson Link provides Pre-GED, GED, and ESL classes. Inmates can enroll in pre-college and college classes in General Education. 25% of the women at Taconic Correctional are enrolled in classes (Hudson Link for Higher Education, 2022).

Prison University Project

The Prison University Project is located at San Quentin Prison in California, a medium-security prison. The program offers an associate's of arts degree through community college. In addition, they offer other courses in humanities, science, English, and math that are usually transferable to a four-year college (Prison University Project, 2022).

Adams State University

Adams State University offers an accredited prison education program through online classes. Students can earn degrees in sociology, business administration, arts, science, and English. In addition, Adams State provides certificate programs in paralegal studies, associate degrees in arts and science, and bachelor's degrees in English/liberal arts, political science, history, interdisciplinary studies, and business administration. The program also has a master's in Business Administration via correspondence education (Prison College Program, 2021).

North Carolina Prisons

The North Carolina Department of Public Safety works in conjunction with the North Carolina Community College system to provide classes in North Carolina prisons. Classes are offered by 49 community colleges at 80 prison facilities. These programs are centered on basic education and technical and vocational training (North Carolina Department of Public Safety, 2019).

Gaston County Prison has classes in character education, Alcoholics Anonymous, Narcotics Anonymous, DART Aftercare, Think Smart, Bible study, religious services, and community leave. At Harnett County Correctional, Central Carolina Community College works with the prison to provide vocational programs such as barbering, carpentry, electrical wiring, food services, masonry, welding, and facility maintenance. Classes in adult education and for preparing to take the HI-SET tests are also available. Inmates may also seek four-year degrees through UNC Chapel Hill Correspondence Courses (North Carolina Department of Public Safety, 2019).

Johnston Community College works with Johnston Correctional to provide vocational classes in masonry, horticulture and food service technology. JCC also provides academic classes in Adult Basic Education and General Equivalency Diploma (ABE/GED). GED testing is available. Human resource development and college correspondence courses are also available. Inmates may also take part in self-help programs such as Alcoholics Anonymous, Narcotics Anonymous and DART aftercare. Substance abuse treatment is provided through NCDPS alcohol and chemical dependency programs and other substance abuse programs including "Big Book Study" and "Twelve-Step Program" (North Carolina Department of Public Safety, 2019).

Within Orange Correctional Facility, Piedmont Community College works with the prison to provide vocational classes in food service technology and light construction. Classes for adult education and preparation for the GED test are available. Individual tutoring is available through the Orange County Literacy Council volunteers who come regularly to the facility. Study release, which allows prisoners to leave the facility and go to classes, is currently available at UNC-Chapel Hill (North Carolina Department of Public Safety, 2019).

Sanford Correctional Facility delivers night programs for inmates, which include Alcoholics Anonymous, Narcotics Anonymous, Yokefellow Bible study and religious services. Central Carolina Community College provides classes for adult education and preparation for GED tests (North Carolina Department of Public Safety, 2019).

Wake Technical Community College works with Wake Correctional Facility to provide full-time vocational classes in certified communications, heating/air conditioning and electrical wiring. Part-time classes in blueprint reading and horticulture are also available. Educational classes in GED, college-level courses and college correspondence classes are available (North Carolina Department of Public Safety, 2019).

Caswell Correctional Facility houses courses through Piedmont Community College to provide vocational courses including welding, HVAC technology, horticulture, and industrial maintenance technology. Inmates with less than a high school education may participate in GED preparatory classes or remedial education (North Carolina Department of Public Safety, 2019).

Bureau of Prison School District

The Federal Bureau of Prisons has begun an education push within their facilities and, with help from the Bonner group, is designing a semi-autonomous school district. The system will offer adult literacy, high school diplomas, and post-secondary education along with education for those inmates with learning disabilities. Inmates will be assessed to determine which educational programs are appropriate. An individualized education plan will be developed and used throughout the inmate's time in prison. A pilot program allows inmates to have blended classes including online components through a special tablet. Second Chance Pell Grants will be used to assist inmates in funding post-secondary education (Bureau of Prisons, Justice, 2016).

Campbell University Sampson Correctional Program

The Campbell University program at Sampson Correctional in Clinton, North Carolina, is another great educational program. The program was begun in 2019 with fifteen members in the first cohort. Many of the participants came from other North Carolina facilities in order to participate in the program. The program is funded through the Bob Barker Corporation and Sunshine Lady. In August 2021, 11 students graduated with an associates of science degree that focuses on academic rigor, faith development, critical thinking, writing, math, and life skills. Many of the graduates attained Dean's List during their studies. Ten out of eleven graduates immediately began their work toward a bachelor's degree in communications, which will focus on substance abuse treatment. This will place graduates in an excellent position to mentor other formerly incarcerated individuals. A new cohort has begun.

Many of Campbell's main campus professors have taught classes in the program. The author had the opportunity to teach the students in the Sampson Correctional program. The students were engaged, talkative, hardworking, and high performing. They seemed to value their education in ways that students on the main campus did not. Some of the thoughts one student had about the program follow:

> The Campbell University post-secondary education program held at Sampson Correctional Institution is truly an "agent of change" within the North Carolina Prison System. In my opinion, this specific educational program is the most fiscally responsible program for tax-payer dollars in the state of North Carolina. Therefore, data suggests that the Campbell University Educational program will effectively reduce the almost 70% recidivism rate for previous offenders within the state of North Carolina for those offenders that partake in the program. Likewise, it just makes logical sense to spend NC tax-payer dollars and private funding to invest in a program that is truly "effective" from a statistical perspective. On the contrary, continuing with the definition of "insanity" (doing the same thing over and over, and expecting a different result), is investing in other "non-effective" programs that do not move the needle in recidivism, and allows additional endangerment to the public's overall safety once the offender is eventually released. Moreover, this educational program not only empowers offenders by providing an opportunity to earn an accredited degree through a well-known private university within the state of North Carolina, but also

truly provides the offender with motivation to become a productive member of society by becoming attractive to employers. Most importantly, this program is unique as there is a collaborative effort between Campbell University, the NC Dept. of Public Safety, Private Donors, and Offenders. Thus, everyone involved is a "stakeholder" in the performance, and ultimately the success of the program. In conclusion, this program is a "win-win" interaction for everyone involved, as the program has a direct correlation on the following factors: safety, fiscal responsibility, recidivism, employability, and a sense of becoming more than what was previously believed one could be. In short, I am humbled and very grateful to partake in this opportunity to earn a better life for myself, my family, and the community in which I will be associated with once I am released to society.

Another student said:

My experience with Campbell's liberal arts program has been truly life changing. Me, as well as many of my peers, come from low-income households; going to college was never even an afterthought for me. I never dreamt that I would have the opportunity to obtain a higher education, FOR FREE, while incarcerated, but I'm certainly eternally grateful for the chance to do so. It makes me feel as if I have a much better chance of "making it" when I re-enter society.

Another participant said:

This program has had a major positive impact on my life. Beginning with my mindset. I never had any intention in becoming a college student, I grew up the only boy in a single-parent home raised by my mother and had to learn second hand how to be a man and do the man duties around the house. By getting into this program, it allowed me to see past what I know and the vast amount of information that I did not know and other things that I did not know that I was good at. So, it took my mindset from a closed mindset to a growth mindset, broadening my spectrum on life and what I as an individual could do to be a productive citizen in society. Through my 2 years in the program my observation is that the idea behind the program was to help me find out who I am and how I can perfect myself. It's a known fact that before you can help someone else you have to help yourself. With that being said, having been through situations leading to my incarceration I feel that I now can help someone that may be heading in the same direction that I was heading in and stop them before it gets to this point. A question I pose to myself and others a lot Is, who better to help someone that has been in a similar situation than a person that has already been through a situation of the same nature? This program is a life changer in so many ways and I don't have enough time to show you all the ways in which it has helped me, however, what my plan to do is upon release take the education that I have learned and apply it to my everyday living and help those in my community which then I hope to have a domino effect on my community.

Another graduate of the program said:

> The program is affecting me in such a great way. I am an aspiring screen writer, and also an inspiring actor/movie director. I'm also excited about the 70 credits that are transferrable to other universities, allowing me to enroll into film school once released. This program has also taught me proper format in my research papers, and overall better writing.

Additionally:

> Coming in the Campbell program, I never really thought that a vocational education would help me progress and be productive. I have always been more into trades and working with my hands. To be honest I really didn't know what a liberal arts degree was; I was mainly influenced to take this program from my longtime friend Nachad Davis who graduated from Campbell law. He introduced me to Professor Jon Powell, and they were so positive they made want to be a part of this program. So, it's safe to say I almost blindly joined off of faith that I would meet similar people, and that's exactly what happened my first semester. I met the most enthusiastic wonderful people, and I am not exaggerating. Dr. Truffin, Dr. Roberson, Dr. Taylor, Dr. Smith, and Dr. Barnes really made me feel capable and like a real student. This program is the most positive thing I've ever seen in prison. I was the librarian for over six years, so I always liked to read, but I have never been taught on this level. Being a person who has always worked with my hands, this program has taught me critical thinking at its best and tools I believe everyone should have and know I can use these same tools and apply them in the workforce even if it is a manual labor job.

Another participant added:

> I am still learning what Dr. Smith and Dr. Truffin expressed as important to our futures going forward: critical thinking. This Campbell University Liberal Arts program has introduced me to a world of concepts and theories, which reinforces critical thinking, and I have grown immensely as a student (and person in general) with this knowledge. There was an article recently published about the students at Sampson, which mentioned a quote from a member of my cohort, who expressed the most memorable literary work he's read in his first semester was Plato's "Allegory of the Cave." I too favored this writing because Plato articulated the plight of a prisoner's mentality so well that it seemed as if he himself has experienced the trauma of imprisonment. From experience, I know that to be released from an oppressive environment does not mean that you are in fact free from its psychological effects.
>
> My first semester at CU provided a foundation for my moral compass going forward, thus I will utilize for the rest of my life. I wasn't a terrible person before I began this program, but I had things to prove. I betrayed the trust of

my community; I am physically apart from my family because of my rash decisions; and I need to have reputable people behind me to prove that I am not only rehabilitated, but that I care about how much I affect my community. I've always wanted to be involved in the politics of my community, and this program introduced me to people and ideas which may support my future political endeavors. The Political Science course with you, Dr. Cowling, both confirmed and challenged many of my political views as a centrist, and I appreciate your candor. My plans are to continue to grow as an individual with information I've learned as a Campbell student. I appreciate each and every professor, administrator, funder, etc. whom contributed to the support of this program because this experience will be key my future success.

Another participant noted:

Your class taught me about the current political structures affecting my personal demographic. Specifically, I learned how the Patriot Act enables law enforcement and courts to sometimes circumvent constitutional rights of individuals to protect the public. Likewise, I learned how law enforcement took advantage of my obliviousness and minute knowledge of US law. In congruence to other social classes, I learned how these systems may be perceived as racist or prejudiced. Succinctly, many of the minority groups in the prison system seem to understand the law only until they're appointed a lawyer, study law by themselves in jail, or study after their sentence. Some critics, however, may argue that it's *their* own fault for not learning about the law or government before incarceration and purposely avoided the resources to learn about it during their schooling years. Thus, current structures pertaining to criminal law seem racist because majority of the incarcerated are ethnic minorities, and uneducated in politics.

Moreover, some paid lawyers prey on client ignorance of the law and sometimes advise them to take bad plea deals to avoid extra work. However, I learned our judicial system is better than those of many underdeveloped and developing countries. Nevertheless, we rank with these same countries in infant mortality rate and other social problems, insulating that we need to continue to work together to overcome structural barriers in these arenas. Also, US law enforcement is able to bypass what we perceive as our protected privacy rights in order to investigate without consent of a judge deeming it necessary. Ultimately, if these points were presented to me before committing my crime, I wouldn't have done it—as I'd weigh these cons more accurately and acknowledge they significantly outweigh the pros.

Now, I hope to disseminate information like this to potential criminals or high-risk children to help them avoid the cognitive, emotional, and physical suffering of incarceration. For example, a wise person told me to sum and divide what I earned from my crime and the time potentially spent in prison to measure its value (impossible because years vary depending on judge and D.A. instead of precedence). But some won't understand this perspective because it's retrospective. A forewarning of probable loss is like a road sign saying, "plutonium poisoning," "radioactive," "deadly." As a result, I insist instead measuring the risk-to-profit ratio like investors because its more salient to individuals like myself with drug crimes—since we have the same mentality for profit gains and losses as legal capitalists. Put another way, many drug traffickers I interviewed during my sentence value their liberty more than illegal profits, whether doing *six* years or *thirty* for the *same* crime with aggravating/mitigating factors.

In addition, I'd tell them pharmaceutical companies are the highest payers for lobbyists to soften government officials, have the largest product-user demographic (with physicians as their forefront), and their product is legal. Therefore, it seems to me they parallel drug cartel tactics in a legal fashion and their products make it to the black markets regardless. As I explain these concepts to individuals, most won't justify drug dealing as equal to the pharmaceutical industry, but rather understand there's a right and wrong way to do the same thing. Put another way, both sides sweat and bleed for their initiatives—objective facts about government create a paradigm change. Thus, a mind-frame dynamic between money and poverty (mostly subjective) changes to liberty and incarceration statistics (mostly objective). Therefore, prevention of drug trafficking won't be caused by incarceration after the fact, but rather understanding that law enforcement and the judicial system are so flawed the reward isn't worth the risk unless you have expensive lawyer money set aside before you commit a drug crime—even though majority of drug offenders wouldn't commit drug crimes if they are already economically stable.

Understanding in general is like peeling layers of an onion to get to the important facts. Now, if we cease to demonize drug selling to the public who don't use or sell them yet will now see two basic choices. First choice: sell drugs and confidential informants may send you through a tough and arbitrary justice system you can't escape from unless you risk your life or have already acquired wealth for a team of paid lawyers—and even then, you may face substantial time. You'll see family suffer and can't do anything about it, have no female companionship, and face time in years you'll immediately regret. The second choice is: Avoid all that, enjoy what prisoners don't—even if you don't have much money—and learn skills to generate intrinsic and extrinsic wealth, knowing people who have been through it all will help you succeed without selling narcotics. Many understand the latter without a doubt, but few understand or perceive the former. Therefore, the goal seems to be to disseminate this information to unreached audiences (the communities facing high drug related incarceration rates).

As an advocate for positive deviance, it appears people have to change since government structures are by far less willing—for profit purposes (seemingly).

> Therefore, I hope to build a rapport with these individuals to help them seek ways to avoid economic crimes by introducing fulfilling alternatives and educational opportunities.
>
> Ultimately, I'll explain the consequences of crime I was oblivious to, using the concepts we learned in your government lectures. For the individuals who are living in that lifestyle, I want to teach them ways to deviate, like others have, to avoid incarceration by investing their earnings on legal businesses before it's too late. For the ones who are tempted to enter that lifestyle, I want to warn them about their probabilities of getting caught and what they'll face when incarcerated. Truly, some people can't fathom the implications of incarceration until they experience them, or until someone takes the time to explain it sufficient detail and expertise.

Finally, another student said:

> This program has had a major positive impact on my life. Beginning with my mindset. I never had any intention in becoming a college student, I grew up the only boy in a single parent home raised by my mother and had to learn secondhand how to be a man and do the man duties around the house. By getting into this program, it allowed me to see past what I know and the vast information that I did not know and other things that I did not know that I was good at. So, it took my mindset from a closed mindset to a growth mindset, broadening my spectrum on life and what I as an individual could do to be a productive citizen in society. Through my two years in the program my observation is that the idea behind the program was to help me find out who I am and how I can perfect myself. It's a known fact that before you can help someone else you have to help yourself. With that being said, having been through situations leading to my incarceration I feel that I now can help someone that may be heading in the same direction that I was heading in and stop them before it gets to this point. A question I pose to myself and others a lot is, who better to help someone that has been in a similar situation than a person that has already been through a situation of the same nature? This program is a life changer in so many ways and I don't have enough time to show you all the ways in which it has helped me, however, what my plan to do is upon release, take the education that I have learned and apply it to my everyday living and help those in my community which then I hope to have a domino effect on my community.

Campbell University has also begun an educational program at Anson Correctional, a women's institution in Polkton, North Carolina, under their Second Chance Initiative. The program partners with Arise Collective. The program is designed to help inmates "develop skills and abilities to contribute to their communities and live upstanding lives." With areas of study in Behavioral Science, Addiction Studies, and Communications studies, the

Campbell University program is designed to help graduates have successful reentry and successful lives after release. They are especially prepared to work with other inmates as counselors and mentors. Participants in the program must have served at least two and a half years, and must meet criteria to be accepted by the university and Arise Collective. The program aims to directly deal with three needs women face upon being released from prison: employment, life skills, and education (Liggett, 2022).

Education can be a major factor in turning the lives of incarcerated individuals around. Education not only reduces the chances of returning to prison, but it also unlocks potential in the students that can ultimately benefit society. It is imperative that we provide these opportunities for the benefit of all.

Chapter 2

Employment

Employment is one of the leading predictors of recidivism for offenders reentering society. Employment, and specifically, steady and reliable employment, is critical to success upon reentry. However, formerly incarcerated individuals face significant hurdles in regard to employment. "Former prisoners occupy an especially disadvantaged position in the labor market, partly because of the characteristics they had prior to being incarcerated and partly because their contact with the criminal justice system has further damaged their job prospects" (Valentine and Redcross, 2015, p. 2). In addition, unemployment adds to the barriers already facing those entering society. "The vast majority [of reentering offenders] encounter difficulties in various areas of adjustment. Employment opportunities, access to government benefits, stable housing, treatment programs, family support, access to health care and a positive parole experience are needed for successful reentry" (Pogrebin et al., 2004, p. 2). This chapter will discuss the research on the relationship between employment and recidivism.

Good examples of employment programs will be described, and the "Ban the Box" movement explored. For those formerly incarcerated, employment programs, employment training, and employment contacts should be offered and used extensively to assist returning citizens to reintegrate into society without reoffending. There is good evidence-based research confirming that an increased rate of employment is associated with a lower rate of recidivism.

Recidivist offenders are likely to be unemployed and either uneducated or undereducated. A five-year follow-up study found that the most important factors in predicting recidivism are employment, age, and education. Education increases the likelihood of employment and reduces the likelihood of recidivism. Employment is the most important indicator of recidivism and, more specifically, employment sustainability is most important in reducing recidivism. Education and job training programs are necessary to increase employment and decrease recidivism (Nally et al., 2014). The system needs to do more here, though there are already many programs.

Many who have been justice-involved find getting employment a difficult task. Because there is tough competition for jobs, those with prior convictions will be ignored. Some recently released inmates apply for many jobs only to receive offers for part-time or temporary jobs at low-paying levels. According to Visher, Debus, and Yahner for the Urban Institute, former inmates need to locate work within two months of release and make more than minimum wage in order to avoid returning to prison. Many are turned away just because of their convictions. Prisons need to do more in regard to job training and connecting those being released with jobs (Visher, Debus, and Yahner, 2008).

Prisoners state that employment is an important factor in staying out of prison, but few have a job lined up upon release. Few inmates get employment-related training. Work release programs and case-managed reentry services have positive impacts upon release. Transportation is also a significant barrier to employment (Winterfield et al., 2009)).

Employment upon release from prison has a direct effect on the return to prison. Those who worked before prison and those who began work shortly after being released from prison had significantly lower recidivism rates (in some cases reducing the rate by half). Those who held a job in prison and those who attended job training programs were more likely to be successful in finding employment. Those who received higher wages at their jobs were also more successful with reentry (8% return for those making more than $10, 12% for those earning $7–10 per hour, and 16% for those earning less than $7 per hour). The recidivism rate was better for all those employed than for those unemployed, which was 23%. In prison, jobs and evidence-based programs are needed (Visher, Debus, and Yahner, 2011).

Prison employment programs do not work equally for all groups of released prisoners. The America Works program provides a work training course that uses “tough love” to teach interpersonal communication, time management, and anger management. The program also teaches resumé preparation, search strategies, and interview techniques. They use partnerships with employers to help employees find and keep jobs. In a study of this program, Yelowitz and Bollinger (2019) found that job placement training substantially reduced the rate of rearrests among nonviolent offenders, from a rate of about 50% to 31%. The same was not true for violent offenders in the training program. For targeted groups, the cost can be worth it.

Criminal justice professionals providing services to ex-prisoners should be aware that the influence of employment on reincarceration appears to diminish over time, and they should continually assess ex-prisoners’ motivation level and incorporate therapy models such as motivational interviewing and solution-focused brief therapy to enhance motivation and goal setting. Furthermore, states, counties, and departments of corrections need to allocate funding to post-release services, including not only employment services but also substance abuse counseling, psychological counseling, family counseling, and/or case management services that could enhance desistance from crime. Although employment alone enables the ex-prisoner to advance to the second stage of the behavioral change process, it apparently may not be enough to engender a permanent change in criminal behavior (Yelowitz and Bollinger, 2019).

Ex-prisoners' employment when released from prison helps to extend their time crime-free in the community. The correctional community and the general public are challenged to recognize desistance from crime as a process and to value interventions that prolong offenders' motivation to remain crime-free. Because most criminologists consider ex-prisoners to be most at-risk for reincarceration during their first year out of prison, existing post-prison services generally target offenders within their first year of release but are virtually nonexistent for ex-prisoners who have been out of prison for more than one year (Travis, 2000). This study indicates that practitioners should offer long-term and continued support to ex-prisoners.

There are some legal protections for former offenders applying for work. An employer may not make or keep records regarding an arrest, detention, or disposition where a conviction did not take place, though this does not apply to felonies. Title VII of the Civil Rights Act of 1964 and the Equal Opportunity Commission makes denial of employment due to criminal record a potential case of racial discrimination. The employer must have a business necessity for the exclusion, which would be based on the nature or gravity of the offense, the time that has passed since the conviction, and the nature of the job sought or held (Aukerman, 2003). In many instances, the offense committed has no bearing on worthiness for a particular job,

Many formerly incarcerated individuals have difficulty finding jobs due to questions on the job application. These might be, "Have you ever been convicted of a crime other than a minor traffic offense?" Or "Have you ever been convicted of a felony?" These questions make it very easy to eliminate people who answer "yes" to the questions, discriminating against those reentering society.

In response to this, the "Bar the Box" movement has arisen. These policies remove these questions from employment applications, particularly when the criminal record has no bearing on qualifications for the job. In 2019, the National Defense Authorization Act prevented federal agencies from seeking information about an applicant's prior criminal record. North Carolina enacted Ban the Box in 2020 to "increase job opportunities for offenders." The law prohibits application questions on prior history, consideration of pardoned or expunged convictions, background checks, and provides applicants with an opportunity to explain any criminal charges ("North Carolina Adopts "Ban-the-Box Law," 2020).

Research confirms that "banning the box" yields more employment for recently released citizens. The National Employment Law project reports that, "after [NDAA], there was a 33% increase in the number of applicants with records hired, which resulted in 21% of all new hires in the district [of Washington DC] being people with records" (Hartman, 2021, p. 2). Research in Durham County, North Carolina, revealed that 98% of those with records get the job they were recommended for after the law was changed. This represents a tripling of the percentage of those attaining jobs over two years (Carper and Hartman, 2021).

There may be a downside to banning the box. Employment in general among Black men and Hispanic men ages 25 to 34 without a college degree actually fell after the passing of "Ban the Box" legislation. Demographics might be being used as a proxy for criminal history, as these groups are statistically more likely to have a criminal record. This means that employers would be less likely to hire candidates from these groups, with or without records. The effectiveness of "Ban the Box" policies continues to be debated. Colorado, New Hampshire, and North Dakota have recently enacted "Ban the Box" policies (Carper and Hartman, 2021).

There are other programs designed to encourage employers to hire offenders. The Work Opportunity Tax Credit gives federal tax incentives for employers who hire former offenders. Many former offenders are unable to get bonded by private bonding agencies, and thus cannot be hired. Bonding agencies can now use the Federal Bonding Program to provide no-cost bonds up to $5000 for employees who are required to be bonded to do their job.

Based on the extant research findings, it is clear that the effect of employment on recidivism does not apply equally to everyone of different ages, gender, and background. The fact that many of the evaluation studies on employment-oriented reentry programs have failed to yield solid positive results should trigger the question of "why not?" As evidence indicates, not every type of job, but jobs of higher quality, will influence recidivism. Therefore, employment-oriented programs should focus on building the technical skills and knowledge of the ex-prisoners and help them to get jobs that are of higher quality. Meanwhile, scarce resources need to be focused on those who are most likely to be affected by (un)employment, specifically younger men. As evidence shows, women of older age are the least likely to be influenced by work (Denver et al., 2017).

GOOD EMPLOYMENT PROGRAMS

CEO Works is a program that is meant to provide job readiness training, transitional employment, job coaching and placement, and retention services.

By participating in at least a one-week job readiness orientation, a participant is qualified to receive "up to four days a week of transitional work on a crew and daily pay." On days participants don't work, they will receive job coaching to help them find jobs. Even after finding a job, support will continue for a year. There are over 6,500 enrollments every year, with over 400 participants working daily, and over 90 transitional crews across the country (Center for Employment Opportunities, n.d.).

How does it work? CEO begins with a week-long "Pathway to Employment" course that prepares the participants for entry or reentry into the workforce. This course offers insight into general workplace practices and "connections between thoughts, feelings, and actions" (Center for Employment Opportunities, n.d.). This course also helps those being released assemble the documents needed to reenter the workforce. Immediate transitional work includes working for state and local governments and community-based organizations. Participants usually spend around three months on a crew prior to "securing unsubsidized employment" (Center for Employment Opportunities, n.d.). With services in New York, Michigan, Tennessee, Pennsylvania, Colorado, Oklahoma, Ohio, and California, crews of 10 work under a CEO site supervisor to provide a range of services. These services include indoor and outdoor services. Indoor services include janitorial work, trash removal, furniture moving, light demolition, processing/separating recyclables, renovation and installation, and stripping, waxing, and buffing floors. Outdoor services include groundskeeping, snow removal, tree maintenance, graffiti and litter abatement, highway maintenance, painting, mowing, and more. Services also include event setup and cleanups. In addition, there are a range of training opportunities from forklift licenses to carpentry training, to mental health first aid trainings. With a range of retention services, the goal is to maintain employment and reduce overall recidivism (Center for Employment Opportunities, n.d.). "A benefit cost analysis of the evaluation results calculated total benefits of up to $3.85 for every $1.00 spent on the program. The majority of these benefits came in the form of reduced criminal justice expenditures and the value of services that CEO participants provided to government agencies in the transitional job work sites." CEO works because it combines: (1) paid, structured work alongside coworkers from similar backgrounds and (2) qualified office staff members helping participants prepare for interviews and job searches (mdrc.org). "These impacts represent a reduction in recidivism of 16% to 22% across the three outcomes" (Center for Employment Opportunities, n.d.).

But research does support the notion that employment can effectively reduce recidivism if employment service providers address individuals' antisocial attitudes and beliefs associated with crime, many of which also affect their ability to succeed in the workplace. Not surprisingly, the findings suggested that participants valued the transitional job, primarily because of the structure it provided them day to day. A small number of participants felt they were receiving training that would help them with future employment, but for most participants, CEO offered a paycheck and a structured routine during a difficult transition period. Participants felt supported by staff members and felt they were receiving advice that applied to both professional and personal challenges they encountered. Few staff members reported giving such advice to participants, which is consistent with CEO's focus on employment. If participants' thoughts and behaviors were influenced by CEO staff members, it was likely an unintentional effect (Center for Employment Opportunities, n.d.). CEO significantly reduced recidivism. The program significantly increased employment in the first year of the study, and the financial benefits far outweigh the costs. CEO's impacts on employment and recidivism were stronger for those who were more disadvantaged or at higher risk of recidivism (Center for Employment Opportunities, n.d.).

Defy Ventures is a program that aims to provide those joining society after prison a "second chance (or a legitimate first one)." The program's goal is to learn and work toward establishing one's own company. Core components of the program begin with an intensive training process that provides online and in-person training for about 10 hours per week. Here, participants learn the basics of entrepreneurship and business. Each week, participants must undergo training sessions, assignments, extracurricular readings, exams, and tough contests. Most participants have families, kids, and financial struggles. Participants also work to put their business idea "on paper" by writing a business plan, financial model, and more. Participants "incorporate their companies, open business accounts, generate promotional materials, and solicit customers." Participants also receive coaching and mentorship from a range of business leaders and investors. Many participants can use skills they had in prior criminal careers to become good entrepreneurs (Baladi, 2017).

The program begins with an introductory training where basics are learned, and business ideas are formed. This is followed by "Defy Academy" which lasts about 12 months and is broken into four sections. The idea of participants' business is expanded upon, while they learn about business development, market research, finances, and more. Participants must write up a 15- to 20-page business plan, prepare financial statements, and compete in competitions judged by professionals with various experiences in the field. These competitions can provide money for the company ideas. One competition, Venture Capital Pitch Competition, can earn a participant up to $15,000. Alumni services are also offered. An alumni program provides a network for those who completed at least one level of Defy Academy (Baladi, 2017).

Defy Ventures boasts a 95% employment rate for released clients, and had a 3.58% recidivism rate in 2016. The program has shown a 1452% growth in clients served in the last three years. The program has spent $3,212,907 in the last fiscal year to serve 931 people. Their staff include 24 mentors with 1,291 volunteers and a board of 10 (Baladi, 2017).

"Defy Ventures is in 30 prisons to date and plans to be active in every prison in America in the next thirteen years. Defy Ventures' graduates have a 95% employment rate once they leave prison, whereas 89% of them were unemployed when they entered. 72% of people who leave prison find themselves back behind bars but only 3% of Defy Ventures graduates re-enter the prison system" (Baladi, 2017).

The Last Mile is a program that aims to teach inmates computer coding. It provides employment opportunities prior to release to cushion the impact of reentry, and it provides real work experience so students have marketable skills post release. The focal points of the program are computer-based skills like HTML, CSS, JavaScript, WordPress, React, and more and are all learned through two six-month cohorts (Full Circle Fund, 2020).

TLM Works is a program that provides participants with expertise in coding and an opportunity to gain real-life experience and assemble a portfolio prior to release. This program takes place in San Quentin Prison, and since the internet is not legally allowed in prisons, the program sets up a sandbox (a fake web) that allows participants to work on projects in a simulated way. The work they complete is on a local server. Any proceeds earned are funneled back into the prison education program. After over a year of training, inmates earn a position and are paid industry-comparable wages. TLM Works allows marketable skills to be learned and personal savings to be held, making preparation for transition, and transition itself, easier (Full Circle Fund, 2020).

The Last Mile helps bridge the gap between incarceration and freedom by pairing in-prison software engineer training with continued mentorship post-release (Full Circle Fund, 2020). The cost for the program is $200,000 per year, which is funded privately and with the sale of prison products like license plates.

To qualify for The Last Mile, the participant cannot have disciplinary infractions for 18 months before applying to the program. In addition, any disciplinary issue can get them kicked out of the program. To date, 50 TLM graduates have been released and none have returned to prison. TLM Works is a partnership with TLM and California Prison Industry Authority, where inmates work for $17 an hour. This type of work experience is much more valuable than making license plates or furniture. TLM participants are able to save for their transition from prison to the outside world (Madrigal, 2018).

A study by Valentine and Redcross (2015) found that transitional job programs were effective in employment in program related jobs and in reducing recidivism. The research examined the Center for Employment Opportunities and the Transitional Jobs Reentry Demonstration. Transitional job programs provide temporary paid work, support services, and job placement assistance. The programs assist participants in developing soft skills needed for employment. They learn by working and work on workplace problems like tardiness and difficulty taking direction that could result in being fired. These transitional programs provide stability and income for former offenders, which is important to future employers. They are better equipped to find a job and more likely to be able to keep a job.

Employment is especially important for those serving terms of parole. They may be required to pay additional expenses relating to their monitoring such as urine analysis, halfway house expenses, restitution, and supervision fees. In addition, many parolees are burdened with expenses such as child support, and debt payments for debts accrued before their incarceration. This makes it more difficult for these offenders to become financially stable. If they are unable to meet the terms of their parole, of course, they will return to prison. Some even choose to flee from parole when they become overwhelmed by their circumstances. This makes finding and keeping successful employment even more critical for these people (Pogrebin et. al, 2014). Employment can mean the difference between success and failure, and it can prevent a return to incarceration. Employment programs must be put in place and encouraged.

Chapter 3

Rehabilitation

Rehabilitation is a goal of sentencing and a philosophy that seeks to change the desire of a criminal offender to offend. In this manner, it is different from other sentencing philosophies that seek to incapacitate, deter, or get retribution but it is more than a philosophy; it is programming as well. Successful rehabilitation of an offender changes their heart and mind to the extent that they no longer wish to offend and do not need to be deterred or incapacitated. Though every program is not equally successful in rehabilitating all participants, these opportunities are integral for successful reentry without returning to prison. They are cost effective, even given those participants who are not successful. It is a philosophy and practice that is well equipped to reduce the return to prison.

Rehabilitation is critical to stopping the vicious cycle of recidivism. Rehabilitation "includes programs that are designed to reduce recidivism among adult offenders by improving their behavior, skills, mental health, social functioning and access to education and employment" (Federal Bureau of Prisons, 2017) Such programs are "one of the best and most cost-effective ways of preventing [prisoners] re-offending, prisoner rehabilitation and can allow prisoners to reintegrate into society, and not just reenter society." Functions of rehabilitation can include job assistance, reintegration into the community and society as a whole, help with physical and mental well-being, and substance abuse treatment. The overall goal and product are a well-adjusted, productive member of society who has the skills and resources to avoid going back into prison. Often individuals coming out of prison lack jobs, money, and social capital to succeed. It can be hard for many at these points to avoid reoffending. Studies support the practicality of rehabilitation programs before and after release. But these programs may lack funding or be shut down (Whelan, 2020). According to Arbour, Lacroix, and Marchand (2021), rehabilitation programs are especially effective when inmates' criminogenic needs are evaluated. Rates of recidivism can be reduced by 9%, and this effect can last up to five years. Participants who gained the most from these types of programs were those who were at medium risk for reoffending and have weak pro-criminal attitudes. These measures support the widespread use of rehabilitation programs.

Rotman offers an excellent statement in support of rehabilitation:

> Rehabilitation offers a constructive way to improve the criminal justice system. Its concern for offenders as whole human beings enriches the state's reaction to crime with a higher notion of justice and leads to a better law. Without rehabilitative efforts before and after their discharge, offenders' grave social and individual problems will usually lead them to further crime. Moreover, rehabilitation improves the criminal justice system by connecting it to the public health, educational and social welfare systems. (Rotman 1990, p. 183)

Andrews et al. (1990, p. 369) add that "Careful reading of the literature on the psychology of criminal conduct and prior reviews of studies of treatment effects suggests that neither criminal sanctioning without rehabilitative service, nor servicing without reference to clinical principles of rehabilitation will succeed in reducing recidivism."

REHABILITATION DEFINED

Rehabilitation focuses on medical and psychological treatment, including substance abuse treatment, to change law-breaking behavior to law-abiding behavior. Treatment is designed to deal with underlying problems that led to criminal behavior. Ideally, those who receive treatment are less likely to repeat criminality. Because prison has many harsh and damaging effects, it is important that there be some element of improving the individual while they are incarcerated. According to Rotman, "In order to neutralize the dissocializing potential of prisons, a civilized society is forced into rehabilitative undertakings. . . . A correctional system with no interest in treatment means dehumanization and regression." 95% of prisoners are released at some point, and the aim of rehabilitation is to prepare former inmates for a law-abiding life on the outside (Rotman,1990).

WHY IT WORKS

There has been much criticism of rehabilitation programs based on their cost and the belief that these programs are not successful. There is, of course, an initial investment in the cost of the program, but there is potential to save money in the long run by reducing future incarceration costs and costs of future crimes averted. There is research finding that while rehabilitation programs initially cost money, these programs end up saving money in the end (Reich, 2017).

In his famous report, Martinson (1974) said "nothing works," but given the context of information we now have about the success of rehabilitation programs (Petersilia, 2011; Cullen and Gendreau, 2001), we now look at "what works." This is referred to as "reaffirming rehabilitation" (Cullen and Gendreau, 2001). According to Cullen and Gendreau (1989), "Nothing works is best seen as a socially constructed reality rather than an established scientific truth."

SUBSTANCE ABUSE REHABILITATION

There is a proven correlation between drugs and crime (McCollister et al., 2004). Within the last 20 years, the population of prisons has grown 200%, largely because of drug offenses (Daley et al., 2004). The larger problem with rehabilitation is convincing the public and politicians that it works and that rehabilitation programs are worth the investment. Estimates in one study indicate up to 30% of male and 20% of female prisoners have drug or alcohol abuse problems. This is much higher than the general population (Fazel, Baines, and Doll, 2006). Drug offenders accounted for 21% of state prisoners and 60% of federal prisoners in 1997. As many as one in six prisoners committed their current offense for drug money. 51% of American prisoners reported using drugs or alcohol during their offense. 83% used drugs in the past, and 57% used drugs in the month before their offense. Assault, murder, and sexual assault were most closely associated with alcohol use (Mumola, 1999).

Using Diagnostic and Statistical Manual (DSM-IV) guidelines for substance abuse or dependence disorders, these disorders were detected in 74% of inmates. Half of subjects were dependent on alcohol or drugs (Peters et al., 1998). As large as the addiction problem is in prisons, treatment is not frequently available for those who need it. While three-quarters of prisoners could be classified as substance-involved offenders, less than one-third reported ever being treated for substance abuse (Mumola, 1999). If the chain of recidivism is to be broken, something must be done to address substance abuse and addiction. This is a critical component of rehabilitation.

While many doubt the efficacy of substance abuse treatment, there is evidence for its success and value. A meta-analysis revealed a relationship between substance abuse and recidivism, and identified risk factors that may assist in prevention. Using a medical model approach, there is hope because addiction is a treatable disease. There are new strategies against addiction that can be used in the criminal justice system (Chandler et. al, 2009).

In the past, the public perception of drug and alcohol treatment programs was negative, but even that is changing. The public understanding has changed, allowing for consideration of treatment. The costs of these programs are small compared to the return on the investment (McCollister and French, 2003). Those making criminal justice policy have begun to follow suit. Policymakers have seen that much crime was committed by a relatively small number of drug-addicted offenders, and that treatment centers could effectively treat these offenders (Wexler, 1995).

The National Institute on Drug Abuse principles for treatment (Chandler et al., 2009) include treating addiction as a behavioral disease. Recovery needs treatment that works with continued care upon release. Treatment should be long enough to make lasting changes in behavior. Participants must be assessed, and treatment protocol should be aimed to meet the needs of the individual being treated. Drug use during treatment should be carefully monitored. Treatment must be aimed at behaviors that are criminal. Corrections staff needs to understand and incorporate treatment policies, and treatment providers must understand the institutional correctional environment. Criminal justice supervision should incorporate treatment planning for drug-abusing offenders, and treatment providers should be aware of correctional supervision requirements. Care and treatment must continue when the patient is released into the community. Both rewards and punishments should be used to achieve behavioral and treatment goals. Offenders with co-occurring drug abuse and mental health problems often require an integrated treatment approach. Medications are an important part of treatment for many drug-abusing offenders (Chandler et al., 2009).

PRISON THERAPEUTIC COMMUNITIES

Sometimes recovery from addiction occurs in a separate environment, the prison therapeutic community (PTC) within prison. A quality definition of a PTC is as follows: "The therapeutic community is a total treatment environment isolated from the rest of the prison population. The primary clinical staff are former substance abusers who themselves were rehabilitated in therapeutic communities. The treatment perspective is that drug abuse is a disorder of the whole person—that the problem is the person and not the drug. A variety of treatment techniques are used, including behavioral, cognitive, and emotional therapies" (Hooper, Lockwood, and Inciardi, 1993).

Therapeutic communities are a residential approach based in the self-help tradition. They teach the notion of a shared problem, the individual as the source of change, the helper-therapy principle, a self-help network to sustain the lifestyle, self-help groups as fixed communities of belief, and self-help processes that develop a sense of power and a fierce independence (Wexler, 1995).

In prison, therapeutic communities are highly structured programs with control over the participants. There are several central features of therapeutic communities: a treatment approach based on treatment philosophy, an atmosphere of empathy and physical safety, qualified and committed treatment staff, clear and unambiguous rules of conduct, ex-offenders and ex-addicts as role models, peer role models and peer pressure, a relapse prevention component, continuity of care from treatment to community aftercare, treatment evaluations, as well as maintenance of program integrity, flexibility, and openness (Wexler et al., 1990).

SUCCESS OF THERAPEUTIC COMMUNITIES

Therapeutic communities reduce recidivism and drug use. Transitional services as patients leave custody are also important. Many more inmates could benefit from therapeutic communities (Harrison, 2001). Daley and colleagues (2004) found when reviewing a therapeutic community, offered through Connecticut's Department of Mental Health and Addiction Services, that for those who were in all of the top three tiers of the program, there were significantly lower levels of rearrest and reincarceration. The Stay N Out program, offered in New York, also provided convincing evidence that prison-based therapeutic community treatment produced significant reductions in recidivism rates (Wexler et al., 1990). Other evaluation studies have shown effectiveness of therapeutic communities as well.

Prison therapeutic communities are effective in reducing rearrest and reincarceration, even without aftercare (Welsh, 2007). The success of therapeutic communities remains significant in reducing relapse and recidivism when including program participation, program completion, and aftercare. Those with aftercare have the best success (Martin et al., 1999). In one prison therapeutic community in Texas, only 25% of those who completed program and aftercare were reincarcerated compared with 64% of program dropouts and 52% of those not in the program (Knight, Simpson, and Hiller, 1999).

The success of therapeutic communities is not without its caveats. Treatment efficacy varies based on the group the individual participates in (Kelly, Welsh, and Stanley, 2019).

One study found no differences in rearrest and reincarceration among those who participated in therapeutic communities and those who did not at the two-year and five-year mark.

While there is a great deal of evidence to support the value of substance-abuse rehabilitation in prison, many argue that the cost of these programs does not justify their use. Taxpayers and the politicians who represent them are hesitant to spend more money to treat incarcerated individuals without proof that their money is being well spent. While not all programs are effective, the general cost effectiveness of therapeutic communities has been demonstrated.

COST EFFECTIVENESS

The Amity Therapeutic Community Program in California yielded a cost effectiveness ratio of $65. It is cost effective (McCollister et al., 2004). The success of therapeutic communities improves with aftercare following release of the participant (McCollister et al., 2003). Washington State found that their Residential Drug Abuse Treatment Program costs $3100 per patient but produces a net savings for each inmate who succeeds of $5200 when accounting for savings of future incarceration costs (Aos et al., 2018). An in-prison therapeutic community was effective in reducing recidivism rates, especially when paired with an aftercare model. Because the likelihood of successful rehabilitation is greater when treatment continues after release, there is a great need for a continuum of care from prison through release and after (Hiller, Knight, and Simpson, 1999). A review of the CREST work release therapeutic community program in Delaware showed that the program resulted in an average reduction of 30 days of incarceration in the future compared to those in regular work release programs (McCollister et al., 2003). These findings make it clear that therapeutic communities are worth the investment and can save future costs of incarceration as well as the reduction of property and personal losses of future crimes prevented. Advocates for prison reform as well as those who wish to reduce crime and recidivism should look to more use of substance abuse rehabilitation in prison settings.

COGNITIVE BEHAVIORAL TREATMENT FOR GENERAL REHABILITATION

Another type of rehabilitative treatment program is cognitive behavioral treatment. Cognitive behavioral treatment is appealing because it seeks to change the measurable traits of thinking and behavior. It is also relatively inexpensive because almost anyone can be trained to provide cognitive behavioral treatment. Cognitive behavioral treatment further targets thinking and behaviors, which are highly correlated with criminal behavior associated with conditions like antisocial attitudes. Cognitive behavioral programs are among the most effective in regard to reducing recidivism among participants (Lester and Van Voorhis, 1997).

COGNITIVE BEHAVIORAL TREATMENT DEFINED

Cognitive behavioral treatment examines the thought processes of criminal offenders. The practice rests in the idea that criminals think differently than those who do not offend and it aims to change those thought processes linked to criminal behaviors. As much criminal behavior is linked to intraindividual problems, cognitive behavioral treatment looks inside the individual to find solutions. Two common models of cognitive behavioral therapy used with offenders are moral recognition therapy and reasoning and rehabilitation. Moral recognition therapy works to change moral reasoning and development; reasoning and rehabilitation programs are aimed at changing how participants process information. Patients examine their own thought processes, specifically victim mentality and blaming the system (Allen, MacKenzie, and Hickman, 2001). Part of the program for Project Reentry while offenders are still incarcerated uses behavioral cognitive therapy to change thought patterns and responses to challenges.

Cognitive behavioral treatment is effective according to Andrews et al. (1990), and Cullen and Gendreau (1989). An evaluation of behavioral cognitive programs was performed by Allen, MacKenzie, and Hickman (2001). Using the Maryland Scale for Scientific Rigor, they evaluated moral recognition therapy and reasoning and rehabilitation and their ability to reduce the recidivism of participants. The study reviewed the strengths and methods of both programs and found that both programs were successful in reducing future incarceration rates.

The risk principle, when applied to cognitive behavioral therapy as suggested by Latessa et al. (2013), states that therapy is not equally effective with all patients. Those at highest risk have the most to gain from the cognitive behavioral approach, while those at low risk may even experience negative effects from exposure to the treatment. Increased time in treatment also increases the likelihood of reducing recidivism. Findings indicated that the "greatest reductions in recidivism were seen in medium and high-risk cases that received between 200 and 249 hours of treatment" (Latessa et al., 2013). This is corroborated by the findings of Andrews and others (1990), who held that treatment is successful when it is delivered to high-risk cases, when it targets criminogenic needs, and when it is matched with client needs and learning styles.

Both addiction treatment and cognitive behavioral therapy are proven methods of rehabilitation. They can reduce the number of former prisoners returning to incarceration. Money and time need to be invested in these opportunities, because they are a wise investment. The takeaway from the rehabilitation research is that various types of rehabilitation therapy can be very beneficial in reducing recidivism. Public support is needed to get past the significant investment needed to bring about true rehabilitation efforts. Ultimately these programs save money and future incarceration.

Chapter 4

Reentry Programs

WHAT ARE REENTRY PROGRAMS?

Around 600,000 prisoners are released from prison each year (Jonson and Cullen, 2015) and many are not adequately prepared to reintegrate into their community. The social costs of this return are great and well beyond the actual criminal activity (Latessa, Cullen, and Listwan, 2006). Reentry has become a part of studying the criminal justice system. This has caused an interest in and study of reentry programs (Jonson and Cullen, 2015). This chapter will define reentry programs, examine their efficacy, and advocate for the use of well-designed reentry programs.

Reentry programs are part of a specific philosophy of successfully reintegrating former prisoners into society. They include "all activities and programming conducted to prepare ex-convicts to return safely to the community and to live as law abiding citizens" (Petersilia 2004, P. 4). Reentry can begin at the very beginning of a prison sentence. Reentry requires the cooperation of community partners, the criminal justice system, families, and victims. Programs typically include assessment, planning, programming, family involvement, employment readiness and discharge planning. (Petersilia, 2014).

Broadly defined, reentry programs focus on the transition from prison to community. Programming can begin in prison and partners with community resources to create continuous care (Seiter and Kadela, 2003). The North Carolina Department of Public Safety says that reentry programs should include the following components: a state reentry council, detailed implementation of a Reentry Action Plan, providing capacity building and technical support to local reentry councils, expanding and formalizing involvement of faith-based and community-based organizations, resolving warrants and pending charges, and addressing major reentry barriers (North Carolina

Department of Public Safety, 2019). A good tool kit for reentry plans should include mental health care, medical care, medications, appointments, housing, employment, substance/alcohol abuse, health care/benefits, income/benefits, food and clothing, transportation, identification, life skills, help with family and children, emergency numbers for assistance, referrals to other services, and a summary of jail- and prison-based medical history.

Reentry programs should be designed to help offenders develop a prosocial worldview, forge positive community relationships, and deal with substance-abuse problems. Specific goals of reentry programs must enable participants to find meaningful employment, locate housing, and to have skills and education necessary to succeed. (NCDPS, 2019).

Pettus-Davis states that five keys for reentry programs are healthy thinking patterns, occupational balance, coping strategies, positive social activities, and strong interpersonal relationships (Pettus-Davis et al., 2019). Successful reentry policy must consider the needs of returning offenders, employers, and the public (Pager, 2006).

Reentry programs are able to shape an offender's behavior as they transition to freedom. They can also deal proactively with former inmates to reduce the return to prison, and help participants to function better for themselves, their family, and their community (Latessa, 2005).

Ideally, reentry preparation should begin immediately upon incarceration. According to Travis, "If John goes to prison, a significant purpose of his activities behind bars would be preparation for reentry" (Travis, 2000, p. 8).

There are three types of reentry programs identified by Seiter and Kadela (2003). First are traditional reentry programs that focus on the transition from prison to community. There are also specific programs offered toward the end of a sentence to educate prior to release. Finally, there are community reentry programs designed to individualize offender management specific to their risks and needs.

REENTRY SUCCESS

Reentry programs reduce recidivism overall, but there are some important issues. Evidence-based strategies are necessary for reentry programming to succeed (Pager, 2006). Not all programs are effective, and some programs can, in fact, increase repeat offending. Programs that follow the risk-need-responsivity model are the most effective. This means that the most successful programs target the most high-risk offenders and provide a continuity of care from incarceration to freedom.

Latessa (2005) cites three core principles for successful reentry treatment. Programs should be focused on high-risk offenders, include cognitive-behavioral or social learning treatment, and have program integrity, which consists of quality assurance and evaluation efforts.

Courts should play an active role in reentry. They can set terms and conditions for release, the same way they do for probation, and set the length of judicial supervision. This can help assure that offenders be supported in their goals for success and that they are held accountable by the court when they are not meeting their goals (Travis, 2000).

Research finds positive results for vocational and work release reentry programs in reducing recidivism and improving job readiness. Halfway-house programs have also been found to reduce both frequency and severity of future criminal behavior. Both sex offender and violent offender programs as well as prerelease reentry programs are correlated with reduced recidivism (Seiter and Kadela, 2003).

TRAVIS'S FIVE PRINCIPLES

In his policy manifesto on prisoner reentry, *But They All Come Back*, Jeremy Travis, a leader in the field, suggests five principles for successful reentry. He advises that all participants in the reentry process must actively pursue these goals. In addition, these goals can be used as a measuring stick for programs and initiatives serving reentering offenders (Travis, 2000).

Travis's five principles are: prepare for reentry, build bridges between prisons and communities, seize the moment of release, strengthen concentric circles of support, and promote successful reintegration. Preparing for reentry is something Travis believes is too often overlooked by correctional institutions. He cites the Ohio Plan as a successful model in preparing for prisoner reentry. This program involves focus on work opportunities (that will translate into work options upon release), health care (including health care benefits and treatment), community roles (resources and safety plan) and personal expectations (Travis, 2000).

Additionally, building bridges between prisons and communities can help deal with the isolation commensurate with correctional institutions. Ties should be created between prisons and other criminal justice agencies to provide a systemic and seamless approach to reentry and limit criminal influences within correctional facilities. Travis recommends civil society—local businesses and religious organizations—should be invited into prisons to open opportunities for employment and spiritual growth. Furthermore, correctional agencies should take a proactive approach by reaching directly into the community to create partnerships (bridges) that provide reentry resources and services for offenders (Travis, 2000).

Travis does not overlook the role of the individual. Those seeking successful reentry must also seize the moment of release. Both formerly incarcerated individuals and partners interested in offender success should not view this critical juncture as the end of the criminal justice process. Rather, both parties should take advantage of this time as an opportunity for offenders to serve the community. Transitional housing, health care, and community ties should be available to offenders to provide alternatives to homeless shelters and crime (Travis, 2000). Transition at the moment of release is critical.

Travis also suggests the importance of strengthening concentric circles of support. Much as it may take a village to raise a child, it may take an entire community to assure an offender's successful transition to a law-abiding citizen. The groups involved in these concentric circles can include the returning prisoner, their family, their peer group, community institutions, social service agencies, and criminal justice agencies. Those closest to the offender and those with sustainable social capital are likely to be more important and effective than state agencies, and the influence has a ripple effect that reaches out to other resources (Travis, 2000).

The final principle among these five is the promotion of successful reintegration. This approach means not only focusing on failures but recognizing successes as well. Long-term success means that eventually the offender will lose the label of offender and become a regular citizen. To encourage this, milestones and victories should be recognized and awarded (Travis, 2000). This creates a step-by-step bridge to success.

RISK ASSESSMENT AND COGNITIVE BEHAVIOR TREATMENT (LATESSA)

According to Ed Latessa, a leader in research in improving prisoner outcomes, researchers have identified a set of principles that should guide correctional programs (Latessa et al., 2013). He recommends focusing on interventions that have been empirically proven to be successful. In other words, practitioners should promote interventions that change offender's behavior. He identifies three proven approaches for achieving successful reentry into a community. This is an evidence-based, or "what works" model.

First, programs must target high-risk offenders for greater success. Latessa contends that studies indicate that low-risk offenders do not need programming because they tend to be more ready for change. Therefore, resources should be focused on high-risk offenders who need programming resources more than their low-risk counterparts (Latessa et al., 2013).

Second, focusing on factors that correlate with crime promotes successful reentry. Risk factors that should be targeted include antisocial attitudes, antisocial peers, substance abuse, lack of problem-solving skills, and lack of self-control. The empirical evidence suggests focusing on non-criminogenic factors, or factors other than those leading to crime such as self-esteem, physical conditioning, and creative endeavors, will not be helpful in reducing recidivism rates (Latessa et al., 2013).

The third principle identified by Latessa is treatment. In short, the most effective treatments are behavioral in nature. Successful behavioral programs focus on present circumstances and are action oriented. Offenders should be demonstrating success as time goes on measured by practical skills, hard and soft. For example, housing, employment, and educational assistance alone will not be successful in reducing recidivism without behavioral changes. Programs that spend time on interventions that are not behavioral are not successful (Latessa et al., 2013). Latessa recommends behavioral cognitive therapy, which is now widely used.

THE PRACTICAL NEEDS APPROACH (GAYNES AND MORANI)

One set of recommendations made by Elizabeth Gaynes in a report for the Annie E. Casey Foundation involves providing services for people who are or have been incarcerated. These recommendations are centered much more around practical needs for reentry and much less around cognitive and behavioral therapy. This approach contrasts sharply with Latessa's (2005) principles. It is, however; an approach quite similar to the services offered at some successful reentry programs. In the report, Gaynes (2005) recommends breaking the suggested services into three phases—incarcerated, about to be released, and formerly incarcerated. Transitions along this journey are key.

For incarcerated people it is essential to "provide needed services and supports related to family, employment, mental and physical health, and spirituality, starting at the point of incarceration to begin planning for release" (Gaynes, 2005, p. 26). Those about to be released need to have a prepared "comprehensive discharge plan that includes living arrangements, medications, identification, transportation, emergency funds, escorts, and linkage to community or faith-based organizations and mentors" (Gaynes, 2005, p. 26). For formerly incarcerated people it is necessary to "make sure these individuals have access to supports and mentoring related to housing, substance abuse treatment, medicine and health care, education, job training, employment, childcare, identification, transportation, and emergency funds" (Gaynes, 2005, p. 26).

Providing more support for Gaynes's approach is the work of Morani et al (2011). They looked at self-identified prisoner needs upon reentry. The study examined 122 former offenders who participated in Project Re-Connect, a six-month voluntary prisoner -reentry program for inmates who served their maximum prison sentence. The needs most frequently self-identified by program participants prior to their return into the community included "transportation, clothing, food, housing, and employment or vocational training" (Morani et al, 2011). These correlate with Gaynes's "practical needs." Meeting these practical needs adds to chances for reentry success.

NO ONE-SIZE-FITS-ALL MODEL (SEITER AND KADELA)

In their study, Seiter and Kadela (2003) found some successes in reentry programs for particular types of offenders. They did not discover a "universal" program model. Different approaches are needed for different offenders. Their findings indicate a positive result for vocational training and/or work release programs (found to be effective in reducing recidivism rates as well as in improving job readiness skills for ex-offenders), for drug rehabilitation (graduates of treatment programs were less likely than other parolees and non-completers to have been arrested, commit a drug-related offense, continue drug use, or have a parole violation), and some success for education programs (only to increase educational achievement scores, but not to decrease recidivism), for halfway house programs (found effective in reducing the frequency and severity of future crimes), and for prerelease programs (effective in reducing recidivism rates of former offenders). Additionally, they report promising results for sex offender and violent offender programs.

INTEGRATED MODEL OF EVIDENCE-BASED PRACTICE (NATIONAL INSTITUTE OF CORRECTIONS)

The integrated model was developed by the Department of Justice and the National Institute of Corrections in response to the huge problem of recidivism. The goal of this effort is to implement evidence-based practices concerning recidivism into all sectors of the adult corrections system. At its heart is the application of principles proven to be effective through empirical research in order to create evidence-based programs. Research should be evaluated and rigorously applied within reentry organizations. Based on the existing literature, the model cites eight basic principles to guide evidence-based programs (Serin, 2005). These principles reflect concepts espoused earlier in the literature review and add to them.

The first step according to the integrated model is to assess actuarial risks and needs of each offender. The assessment tools should consider each offender's specific risk (Guevara and Solomon, 2009). The second step is to enhance each offender's intrinsic motivation. This involves creating an atmosphere that encourages the offender to seek change and understand the difference between their actual behavior and their desired behavior (Crime and Justice Institute, 2009). The third step involves specifically targeted interventions, meaning that the treatments should be suited to each offender's specific needs. Evaluating the offender's targeted interventions includes examining the offender's risk, their criminogenic needs, offender's responsivity, proper dosage, and cognitive behavior treatment (Serin, 2005). The fourth step for successful programs involves trained workers delivering cognitive treatment to address antisocial issues, social learning, and proper communication (Serin, 2005). The fifth step is increasing positive reinforcement to ingrain new behaviors (Serin, 2005). The sixth step requires facilitators to engage ongoing support in natural communities. This is known as the community reinforcement approach and has been proven to sustain positive new behavior (Serin, 2005). For the seventh step, offenders should be routinely assessed and evaluated to make changes and improvements (Serin, 2005). Finally, the eighth step envisions that feedback from the measurements in step seven should be given to employees so that adjustments can be made (Serin, 2005).

WHAT WE LEARN FROM THE REENTRY LITERATURE

From each of these authors we gain some valuable perspective about "what works" in reentry. Many common themes run throughout their work. What we gain from Travis is community involvement and support. What we gain form Latessa is a focus on behavioral and cognitive treatment and risk assessment. Gaynes shows us the importance of emphasis on practical resources for housing, education, and healthcare. Seiter and Kadela give an understanding that certain programs/interventions are successful for some offenders, but there no is one-size-fits-all-approach. The Crime and Justice Institute's integrated model is the best and most complete model and encompasses aspects from each of the other programs and adds program assessment, feedback, and adjustment. It makes logical sense that a combination of community involvement, behavioral and cognitive treatment, practical living resources, individually tailored interventions, and program assessment could be the key to a successful program. Therefore, evidence-based programs should include the following:

1. Behavioral and cognitive treatment

2. Resources for housing, education, health care, and employment
3. Community involvement and support
4. Risk assessment and individualized interventions
5. Program assessment, feedback, and adjustments

This creates a great toolbox of interventions to assist those reentering.

REENTRY COURTS

Jeremy Travis (2000) believes that a good reentry structure should involve judges as reentry managers rather than parole boards and officers. He encourages reentry courts. This would begin with the judge following the reentry progress in prison. After release, the judge would inform the offender of expectations and oversee the sentence with help from other criminal justice agencies. Other participants from the community would be put into place to help ensure the offender's success. Along the way, the offender would have goals to meet, and hearings would be held with the judge periodically to measure success of the offender and to be sure that criminal justice agencies are accountable as well. Milestones that the offender reaches toward reintegration will be acknowledged in court. Family and friends can be brought in to support the offender through their progress. When the offender fails to make good progress, their freedom can be curtailed, but only to the extent necessary. At the end of the program, a graduation ceremony would be held and official status, such as voting rights, can be restored (Travis, 2000). There is a lot of work involved in such a program, but the benefits are great. These types of projects have proved successful in other areas such as veterans' courts, mental health courts, and drug courts. They could be used as an umbrella to oversee offender reentry.

PROJECT RE-ENTRY

Project Re-entry was begun as a North Carolina Community–Department of Public Safety partnership. In 2003, the North Carolina Governor's Crime Commission funded Project Re-entry as a pilot program to provide pre- and post-release services to offenders in Forsyth County and Forsyth Correctional Facility. Today, Project Re-entry assists offenders and former offenders in their transition to society in Buncombe, Cabarrus, Caswell, Davidson, Davie, Edgecombe, Forsyth, Henderson, Halifax, Iredell, McDowell, Nash, Northampton, Rockingham, Rowan, Stokes, Surry, Wilkes, Wilson, and Yadkin Counties. Project Re-entry has served 2,962 offenders with pre-release programs, 869 offenders with pre- to post-release programming, and 2,913 with post-release-only programs (Project Re-entry, n.d.).

The mission of Project Re-entry is to "establish a coordinated system of pre- and post-release services between the North Carolina Department of Public Safety, community resource agencies, the One Stop systems, faith-based initiatives, employers, community residents, and former offenders to reduce criminal justice costs, improve the reintegration of former offenders, and increase public safety." The key components of Project Re-entry include pre-release programming, pre- to post-release programming, post-release-only programming, and community and employer outreach (Project Re-entry, n.d.).

Pre-release programming for Project Re-entry involves a 13-week class for inmates having less than 18 months remaining on their sentence. Programming is currently offered in 13 NCDPS institutions. The goals of this pre-release program include transition realities, attitude in reintegration, deinstitutionalization counseling, job search and readiness skills, accessing resources, building healthy relationships, coping with societal changes, and self-esteem (Project Re-entry, n.d.). Participants develop hard and soft skills.

A typical curriculum for the pre-release program would include classes on attitude and reintegration, victim and awareness, transitional housing, current needs and needs upon release, personality and vocational assessments, community resources and services, employment after release, taking care of yourself (health care), thinking beyond the wall and beyond your criminal record, rescuing and enabling, relationships, budgeting and finance, and keys to making it on the outside. At the end of the program, there is a graduation ceremony with a motivational speaker (Project Re-entry, n.d.).

Pre- to post-release services provided by Project Re-entry help offenders to plan for their release. After graduating from the pre-release program, offenders will have a one-on-one meeting with Project Re-entry prior to their release. The offender will design a home plan, and complete goals and assignments to prepare for release. Post-release appointments are scheduled within 24 hours of release in order to begin post-release services. Among participants in the pre- to post-release program, 100% received case management assistance, 45% received counseling, 94% received personal assistance, 94% received vocational or educational assistance, and 43% received employment assistance (Project Re-entry, n.d.).

Project Reentry offers a variety of post-release services. Typically, offenders are monitored by a case manager for a least one year after their release. They are also mentored by other participants who wish to give back to their community. Specific services offered by Project Re-entry during the critical post-release phase include job readiness and job retention classes, assistance with job search and placement, transitional housing referral, counseling services, vocational and educational services, faith-based or community advocacy/support referral, and personal assistance. For those receiving post-release services only, 100% received case management assistance, 24% received counseling, 66% received personal assistance, 91% received vocational or educational assistance, and 51% received employment assistance. Among their pre- to post-release participants from July 2003 to December 2011, Project Re-entry records a recidivism rate of 12.8%, and among those participants receiving post-release services only, a 15.2% recidivism rate was recorded for July 2003 to June 2010 (Project Re-entry, n.d.).

The successes of Project Re-entry have been noted and rewarded. This includes the 2002 Innovation Award from the National Association of Development Organizations. In 2006, Project Re-entry was cited as a "best practices" program by the US Department of Justice and the Urban Institute. The program also received a 2012 Outstanding Criminal Justice Program Award from the National Criminal Justice Association (Project Re-entry, n.d.).

HOW PROJECT RE-ENTRY MEETS THE GOALS OF EVIDENCE-BASED REENTRY PRACTICE

A comparison and analysis focused on Project Re-entry's ability to achieve each of these five components. Its intent is to gauge Project Re-entry's performance in the five areas that have been determined to be essential for evidence-based programs.

As stated earlier, the five goals of evidence-based reentry programs include behavioral and cognitive treatment; resources for housing, education, health care, and employment; community involvement and support; risk assessment and individualized interventions; and program assessment, feedback, and adjustments. Project Re-entry provides services for their clients that meet each of the five criteria. The following discussion explains how these goals are met, some more successfully than others.

Project Re-entry provides behavioral and cognitive treatment in several ways. Project Re-entry provides its clients with Totally Responsible Person (TRP©) instruction, a practical variation on cognitive behavioral training. Each member of Project Re-entry staff who administers this education is a certified TRP© instructor. Qualified guest speakers are also included in the TRP© program (Howell, 2013).

In addition to providing TRP© classes, Project Reentry assists in referring clients who need additional assistance in the area of behavioral and cognitive treatment. Sometimes Project Reentry staff assists the Department of Public Safety with post-release mental health treatment coordination for serious cognitive and behavioral issues, Project Reentry will call upon community resource partners in order to get treatment for clients from appropriate providers (Howell, 2013).

Finally, Project Re-entry serves as a coordinator for the Treatment for Effective Community Supervision (TECS) program in some counties within its program's jurisdiction. TECS provides cognitive and behavioral and substance abuse treatment for post-release offenders who are eligible under the Justice Reinvestment Act (Howell, 2013).

The second goal for evidence-based reentry programs is to provide housing, education, and employment services. For services in these areas, Project Re-entry partners with community organizations to provide these services to clients. To provide post-release housing for clients, Project Re-entry coordinates pre-release interviews for transitional housing. Project Re-entry also screens potential housing for their clients to make sure that it has a healthy structure and environment to encourage success (this is necessary due to the fact that there is currently no formal oversight or regulation of transitional housing) (Howell, 2013).

In order to provide for the educational needs of their clients, Project Re-entry works with community colleges and workforce partners to provide GED instruction, skills training, diplomas, and trade certifications. Project Re-entry also assists with financial aid through scholarship applications, FAFSA (free application for federal student aid) applications, and financial assistance through the federal Workforce Investment Act (WIA) (Howell, 2013).

Health care concerns for Project Re-entry clients are managed through partner agencies such as the Community Care Clinic. Clients who are referred to such resources as the Community Care Clinic can get free medical exams and services. In addition, organizations such as the Lions Club and the Division of Services for the Blind provide free eye exams and eyeglasses (Howell, 2013).

Great emphasis and importance are placed on employment at Project Re-entry. The program offers direct services in the areas of job search training and support, job retention education and training, interview techniques, interview techniques specific to former offenders (addressing their criminal records), resume development, job readiness, and retention workshops. In order to help secure employment for clients, Project Re-entry develops and maintains relationships with community employers. In addition, they provide Employment Assistance Services to employers. Employment Assistance Services is an on-call support service that an employer can use if there are any questions or concerns that they may have about one of the participants that they have hired. Project Re-entry provides information to employers about incentives such as federal bonding, work opportunity tax credits, on-the-job training, and work experience (Howell, 2013).

The third component of successful reentry is community involvement and support for reentry efforts. In this area, Project Re-entry has been highly successful in engaging community partners to assist in their efforts. Project Re-entry is the primary representative of reentry and transitional programming in the areas they serve. As noted above, Project Re-entry has formed partnerships with community organizations such as local community colleges, Community Care, and Division of Services for the Blind to provide services for clients in the areas of behavioral and cognitive treatment, housing, education, health care, employment, and individual and personal needs (Howell, 2013).

Additionally, Project Re-entry is involved in giving back to the community in several ways. Their efforts include partnerships with other organizations on the 10 Year Plan to End Chronic Homelessness, Project Safe Neighborhoods (a national violence reduction law enforcement initiative), serving as members of local prisons' Community Resource Councils, participation in various employment fairs and career expos, and conducting local, county, and state-wide exhibitions and seminars addressing former offenders and various related issues such as the needs of children of incarcerated parents (Howell, 2013).

The fourth area of evaluation for a successful reentry program is the use of risk assessments and provision of individualized interventions based on those risks. While the participant is incarcerated, the Department of Public Safety completes a battery of diagnostics and assessments on prisoners as part of their intake procedures at the beginning of their incarceration. Individuals are then recommended to specific post-release programming and resources as a result of these evaluations.

Because the Department of Public Safety performs a risk (of re-arrest) assessment, Project Reentry does not specifically assess participants, Project Re-entry provides individualized case management, goal setting, and support as part of their pre-release programming based on specific risks. At the time of the inmate's release, initial post-release visits are scheduled on the day of release or the day after release. The initial post-release visits create an immediate bridge from the pre- to post-release environment that gives participants a sense of structure and safety, "a place to go." In these meetings, the participant's individual case plan is reviewed and refined and includes specifics related to vocational, educational, counseling, treatment, transportation, housing, family, and personal needs. The participant is then given an action plan that incorporates life goals and objectives with program-paid or facilitated services such as employment training, skills classes, educational or certification training, relapse prevention counseling, and personal assistance services (Howell, 2013). These immediate post-release meetings are necessary because the time just after release is critical for success.

The fifth and final area for evidence-based practice is program assessment, feedback, and adjustment. All Project Re-entry participants complete an evaluation of Project Re-entry programming and their overall view on what was good, what should be included that was not in program, and would they recommend the program to others. Based on this feedback, modifications to presentation content and presenters are made to ensure the concerns and needs of participants are met with the most effective presentation format and materials (Howell, 2013). In addition, outside research was conducted to determine the strengths and weaknesses of Project Re-entry.

Project Re-entry staff also use information from the Department of Public Safety's (DPS) formal Risk-Needs Assessment in determining case management needs for those individuals referred to the program while under the Division of Community Corrections (DCC) supervision after release. Project Re-entry staff in some areas also administer the Substance Abuse Subtle Screening Inventory (SASSI) screening tool for post-release participants beginning in fall 2013.

Reentry programs are important to national efforts to reduce recidivism. They need to have many different approaches and tools available for varying types of offenders. Programs should be widely available and aimed at those who could benefit most.

Chapter 5

Faith, Family, and Community

FAITH-BASED PROGRAMS

Prison programs with a basis in a faith tradition provide practical assistance to returning prisoners while using faith-based programming to encourage rehabilitation and change. This is not a new concept, as historically, religion has been a part of reforming and rehabilitating inmates. The idea has had a resurgence recently (Dodson et al., 2011). Though defining what a faith-based program is, and exactly what it contains might be difficult, there are some common elements with faith-based initiatives. There is an element of religious instruction and guidance that does not exist in other programs. "Faith based initiatives can best be described as social programs that are administered by an organization with some type of religious affiliation" (Dodson et al., 2011, p. 367). They are another great tool to reduce recidivism and facilitate rehabilitation.

Sometimes faith-based programs are funded by religious organizations, but not always. They might include spiritual retreats, scriptural study, prayer, and worship opportunities. They may come from many different religious and denominations, backgrounds, and traditions. "Corrections-related faith-based programs offer the potential to reduce the cost-of-service provision through the contributions of committed volunteers" (Bright and Graham, n.d., p. 1). They often include practical needs in their approach and rely on private, non-taxpayer funding (Mears et al., 2006, Bright and Graham, n.d., Young et al., 1995). "Faith groups, with little or no cost to taxpayers, provide many crucial services, both in and out of prisons" (Head and Deroche, 2017). According to Dodson and colleagues (2011), faith-based initiatives work to reduce recidivism. Though there may not be a great deal of research on faith-based programs, the data available suggests a positive correlation between religious initiatives and reentry success (Johnson, 2004).

PRISON FELLOWSHIP

One of the most famous faith-based programs for former offenders is Prison Fellowship. Prison Fellowship was formed by former Watergate offender Charles Colson in 1976 to help incarcerated individuals. Prison Fellowship is now in 88 countries around the world. The program is designed to spread the Christian message and offer a holistic approach to reentry.

Prison Fellowship has several programs to assist inmates and those recently released, which include Prison Fellowship Academy. The Academy provides 12 months of classes before release and referrals for services after release. Classes cover criminogenic risks and needs, such as eight basic thinking patterns and irresponsible attitudes and behaviors that contribute to crime. Students also discuss relationships, the roles and relationships of family members, and the role of feelings in behavior. Life skills and reentry programming address skills needed such as financial management, healthy habits, legal issues, and employment. Participants will also address ways to deal with addiction and recovery issues as well as spiritual formation and Biblical principles. They are taught to "lead lives of purpose and productivity outside of prison" (Prison Fellowship, n.d.).

Prison Fellowship also offers a series of ten workshops specifically for women, called Create New Beginnings. The program is a restorative art program in which the inmates work together creating art in a space that allows them to access and deal with emotions and find self-awareness using artistic expression. They are encouraged to develop healthy relationships through their artwork and through scripture discussions (Prison Fellowship, n.d.).

Hope Events were created by Prison Fellowship to provide special praise and worship opportunities for prisoners. At these praise and worship events, speakers, musicians, and special guests provide spiritual encounters and an opportunity to hear the gospel in a powerful way. In 2020, before COVID-19, nearly 20,000 prisoners attended Hope Events. These events continued during the COVID pandemic through "watch parties" and livestreamed events. These events have been taken to some of the worst prison facilities, including Rikers Island Detention Facility (Prison Fellowship, n.d.).

Families of prisoners are also cared for through the Angel Tree program sponsored by Prison Fellowship. Many children of inmates may not get visits with or presents from their incarcerated parent. Through partnerships with individuals, churches, and other organizations, Angel Tree provides a gift, support, and a Christian message for children from their parent in prison. The Angel Tree programs include Angel Tree Christmas, Angel Tree Camping, and Angel Tree Sports Clinic (Prison Fellowship, n.d.).

Prison Fellowship also formally advocates for justice reform, focusing on a restorative justice approach, which seeks to put all parties back to their pre-crime state. These resources are designed to equip those influencing policy and restorative justice advocates to bring about change at both the state and federal level. They offer small-group curriculum and virtual study groups to engage conversation on restorative justice initiatives. A statement on restorative justice, called the Justice Declaration, is being prepared to send to the president (Prison Fellowship, n.d.).

Wardens are an important factor in prison culture, so Prison Fellowship offers a Warden Exchange course. The seven- to-nine-month programs allows wardens to collaborate with leaders from other disciplines to encourage leadership, moral rehabilitation of prisoners, and community engagement. They become part of a peer network to make prisons safe and restorative and assist inmates with successful return to their communities. These warden graduates act as CEOs of their facilities and reimagine prison life (Prison Fellowship, n.d.).

EFFECTIVENESS OF PRISON FELLOWSHIP

At least one study (O'Connor et al., 2018) has documented the effectiveness of Prison Fellowship. The program was studied for 11 years between 1975 and 1986. Prison Fellowship programming, specifically a two-week conference for previous or former offenders, was found to have a significantly lower rate of recidivism among participants compared to a control group of inmates who did not participate. Recidivism dropped by 11% from the control group, from 51% to 40%. Graduates of the program "were arrested at a slower rate following release from prison [and] maintained a higher survival rate for a longer period of time" (O'Connor et al., 2018).

Additional research (Johnson, 2004) found no difference between graduates of Prison Fellowship and nongraduates in measures of rearrest and recidivism. However, inmates who were most active in Prison Fellowship Bible studies were less likely to be arrested during a three-year follow-up period. Johnson (2004, p. 11) concludes that "Recent research on prisoner reentry indicates that religious institutions and other faith-based organizations should not be overlooked as important pieces of a more comprehensive strategy in achieving successful transition."

In a study of a Prison Fellowship program that trains inmates to be peer mentors, the effect was significant. Those who were trained in a two-week seminar to serve as peer mentors to fellow inmates had significantly lower recidivism rates during the eight- to fourteen-year follow-up period. In addition, the participants had a higher survival rate than those in the control group. Particularly useful is the finding that the program had a greater impact with lower-risk inmates, white inmates, and female inmates. This seems to indicate that the program is more successful with some groups than with others (Sells et. al., 2020).

INNERCHANGE FREEDOM INITIATIVE

Innerchange Freedom Initiative (IFI) was a special program within Prison Fellowship that was started in Texas's Carole S. Vance Unit in 1997, in a partnership with the Texas Department of Criminal Justice. Other sites were opened, for men and women, including sites in Minnesota. This program provides "educational, values-based services to prisoners on a voluntary and noncompulsory basis" (Prison Fellowship, n.d.). The InnerChange Freedom Initiative was a privately funded program that provided educational, values-based services to prisoners on a voluntary and noncompulsory basis to help prepare them to reenter the workplace, religious and community life, and family and social relationships. The program was based on Christian principles but was open to all faith backgrounds. The program provided wraparound services for inmates with 18 months of mentoring and programs during incarceration, followed up by 12 months of support for the newly released inmate in the community. The program was based on a restorative justice philosophy and emphasized offender accountability and victim restoration (Prison Fellowship, n.d.).

IFI emphasized life-skills training, academic instruction, job preparation, community-service opportunities, chapel and Bible studies, support groups, and mentoring relationships. The IFI programs specifically focused on instilling six important personal values needed for successful reintegration into society. These include integrity (living honestly with self and others), restoration (mending relationships with God, families, and community, including victims, when appropriate), responsibility (accepting ownership of choices, behaviors, and their consequences), fellowship (working together to make a healthy, infraction-free community), affirmation (giving and receiving honest feedback and encouragement), and productivity (learning the value of work, education, and contribution to the community). Volunteers work with inmates to provide the programming. The program was renamed Fellowship Academy in 2016. Fellowship Academy boasted highly successful recidivism statistics (Boyd, n.d.). Based on all recidivism research, this provides a balanced approach.

Effectiveness of Innerchange Freedom Initiative

Among 177 Texas IFI graduates released prior to 2000, the recidivism rate was 8% after two years, compared to 19–22% for those who did not participate. Interestingly, those who began the program but did not complete it actually had a higher rate of recidivism of 36% after two years. Mentors after release were especially helpful in reducing recidivism (Trusty and Eisenberg, 2003). A study of Minnesota IFI graduates released between 2003 and 2009 showed that the program significantly reduced rearrest, reconviction, and reincarceration. In addition, the program was cost-effective, as it reduced future incarceration costs, saving about $8,300 per inmate participant. Faith-based programs are effective when they are evidence-based and provide behavioral intervention (Duwe and Johnson, 2013).

OTHER FAITH-BASED PROGRAMS

The Horizon Program at Marion Correctional Institution in Ohio began in 2000. Volunteers are not from one faith but represent Christians, Jews, and Muslims. The program is designed to help inmates develop pro-social beliefs and skills. Mentors assist those in the program for at least two years before they are released. The participants live in interfaith families and learn basic life skills. The program has a very low (14%) recidivism rate for its graduates (Bright and Graham, n.d).

Lawley Correctional Institution in Florida created special faith-based housing for inmates in their facility. Inmates have four hours each month of faith-based self-improvement focusing on life skills, mentoring, and personal integrity. They police themselves, and disciplinary problems mean a transfer to another facility. Inmates housed in these types of units have lower reincarceration rates than comparable groups in other housing settings. One study showed that none of the inmates released after being in a faith-based housing setting were reincarcerated within six months (Bright and Graham, n.d).

Home for Good Oregon focuses on successful community reentry throughout all of Oregon. The program accepts clients from all faiths and is based on a restorative justice model that includes the community in reentry. Chaplains are provided to participants both in prison and within the community. The program administrators believe that community support lowers recidivism, though there no hard data on Home for Good Oregon yet (Bright and Graham, n.d).

In East Harlem, New York, the Ready4Work program is funded by both religious and government sources. Participation in the program's spiritual components is not mandatory. Volunteers from the faith community serve as mentors and have meetings with participants each week. The focus is on work as a route to success for the 400–500 formerly incarcerated individuals served each year. They gain resume-building and interview skills and other tools to assist in gaining employment (Bright and Graham, n.d.).

The Rational Emotive Spiritual Therapy (REST) Inmate Restoration and Aftercare Program provides cognitive therapy and spiritual intervention. There are 13 weeks of sessions during confinement, and a mentor helps connect the inmate with community faith-based groups to direct them to community resources as part of aftercare. Among participants, 84% said the program was helpful to them (Bright and Graham, n.d).

Faith-based initiatives offer great hope in improving outcomes for recently released offenders. While more research needs to be done, these programs appear to reduce recidivism and its cycle. Though there are legal and funding issues, faith-based instruction should be readily available as an option or reentry success. Their benefit should not be overlooked.

Chapter 6

Social Capital, Peers, and Other Practical Needs

Social capital is a necessary tool for successful reentry and for reducing recidivism. Social capital is the ability to draw upon resources from friends, family, and community. It is defined as "networks, shared norms, values, and understandings that facilitate cooperation within or among groups and access to important resources" (Flavin, 2004, pg. 209), and is critical for the formerly incarcerated. Social capital helps with resocialization and development of reciprocity, trust, and cooperation. It can also help those returning to find practical resources needed for reentry. Social capital can open doors of opportunity and provide assistance with specific needs like housing and employment (Smith and Hattery, 2011). Social capital is the ability to accomplish goals through use of community resources.

Families can be critical sources of social capital for returning citizens for two reasons. First, family ties tend to be more long-lasting than other forms of connections. Second, families are helpful in connecting members with needed resources outside the family network (Flavin, 2004). Prisoners who maintain strong relationships with family while incarcerated lower their risk of reincarceration, and those relationships assist greatly with reentry needs. "Importantly, the maintenance of 'good quality' relationships during a prison sentence has been associated with the successful development of the relationship post release" (De Claire and Dixon, 2017, p. 185). While more work needs to be done, the existing research suggests that maintaining high-quality relationships while in prison is critical for reducing recidivism and for reentry: "Since rehabilitation and re-entry of the offender into the community is the ultimate goal of the correctional system, it should be obvious that the maintenance of the offender's family system is of vital concern," (De Claire and Dixon, 2017, p. 185).

Prisoners know that help from family is important to successful reentry. Most inmates have some contact with family on the outside, but few get visits. Often distance from family makes visiting difficult. Family support has been shown empirically to reduce recidivism and improve employment prospects, as it improves social capital. Most prisoners return to a few neighborhoods within a few cities, which are socioeconomically disadvantaged. Those who relocate often move to areas similar to those they left. When they return to these communities, they are at greater risk of recidivism (Project Re-entry, n.d.).

Family is a key component of success in reentry. Those who have frequent contact with the families during incarceration have greater success and less recidivism upon release. But many parents behind bars don't get regular visitation with their families because of scheduling difficulty, distance, cost, and inhospitable facilities. Some prisons do have programs to improve parenting skills, but there is a need for more.

Social contacts in the community are critical as well. Those who are newly released lack structure and social contacts. They are also unfamiliar with new technologies. The communities that inmates come back home to are more disorganized and have higher rates of crime and unemployment.

Peer networks are another form of social capital which may be available for prisoners returning to the community. Although more research is needed, research indicates that peer mentorship programs reduce recidivism rates. While some peers can be negative influences, peer mentors may have a positive impact. The way that this occurs is unclear. In a review of Second Chance Act Peer Mentoring, Sells et al. (202) found that peer mentorship was successful in reducing recidivism and provided a source of needed informal socialization. These programs can provide psychosocial support, transitional services and community resources. Peer mentorship programs that focus on early intervention, relationship quality, criminal desistance, social navigation, and gainful citizenship assist participants in overcoming criminogenic obstacles. Peers can help to re-socialize successful mentees (Sells et al., 2020).

A 2015 study found that peer mentors can assist with obtaining identification, enrolling in substance abuse treatment, community college, and finding transportation, employment, and housing. Those who were mentored benefitted greatly and the return to prison was reduced significantly. One mentee said, "It's motivation because I can see somebody that was in the same place with me . . . and then for him to be there to help me with my problems. . . . It makes me inspired and motivated to have someone like him seriously in my life" (Marlow et. al, 2015, p. 97). Not all mentors are equally successful. Among the characteristics that were deemed most important for mentors to have were: a history of incarceration and reentry, overcoming trauma, history of addiction and recovery, and similar age, race, and gender. The most important characteristic among these, according to mentees, was a prior experience with incarceration (Matthews, 2021). Actions of peer mentors that are important include caring, listening, encouraging, and managing small goals (Buck, 2018). "Peers operate like caseworkers except that they use and apply their lived experience to aid others" (Reingle Gonzalez et al., 2019, p. 1872). Mentees need to know that mentors understand their struggle to make them credible. It is difficult to understand and relate if the mentor has not experienced the situation.

Peer mentor networks have reciprocal benefits for mentors as well as mentees. Peer mentors serve as role models and can be experts with experience in ways those who have not been incarcerated cannot have. The work can give mentors hope for the future, civic reintegration, and a new prosocial identity. It reminds them of a path they do not wish to go down again, and it can strengthen their resolve. It contributes to humanizing offenders in roles of both mentors and mentees (Nixon, 2020). These relationships foster a prosocial sense of belonging and accountability.

Similar positive effects have found for programs for female offenders (Goldstein et al., 2009) and veterans (Simmons et al., 2017). The many benefits can be summarized as follows: "First, peers tend to offer practical help; second, relationships between the peer and the recipient may involve self-disclosure and friendship; and third, peers can offer hope as a result of having experienced similar issues" (Simmons et al., 2017, p. 647). These programs should be enthusiastically promoted.

PRACTICAL NEEDS

The Urban Institute identifies the main practical needs for successful reentry as: basic needs (transportation, clothing and food, financial resources, and identification and important documents), housing, employment and education, health care (physical illness, mental illness, and substance abuse), and support systems (La Vigne et al., 2008). North Carolina's Department of Public Safety has identified four practical needs that returning citizens must deal with. These include transitional employment, transitional housing, transportation, and substance abuse and mental health treatment (North Carolina Department of Public Safety, 2019).

While these things can greatly improve the chances of successful reentry, often formerly incarcerated individuals lack access to them. There are successful programs to help returning citizens with these issues, such as Oregon Department of Corrections program to help obtain financial resources, the HIRE network, Idaho's Transition and Treatment Funding Program, and the Mass Health Pilot Program. In other areas, recently released people may not have resources available. According to the National Conference of State Legislatures (2023), some state have assistance in place to provide access to health care for recently released prisoners but others do not. While obtaining proper identification is critical to obtaining a job and housing, completing the necessary process can be time-consuming and expensive. While some states, including Texas and Ohio, provide help in this area, many do not, and tracking of the available resources is difficult (Wise, 2020). Increased access to practical needs resources must be provided.

INTERVIEW WITH AN INMATE ABOUT PROGRAMMING AND SOCIAL CAPITAL

Tony is an engaging man, who makes frequent eye contact and expresses himself very eloquently. He began by talking about his experiences in prison. He went to prison at 16 years old and was incarcerated for approximately 17 years in medium and closed facilities, including five years at Sampson Correctional in Clinton, North Carolina. He received no family support while he was in prison; his mother made that clear when he was convicted. He was released around 2012.

While he was in prison, Tony occupied his time in several ways. He worked with dogs, went to anger management classes, took coaching classes and vocational rehabilitation, got his GED, and even went to classes, but only for the food, since he has never had any substance abuse issues. He was fully committed to his GED classes and is very glad that he participated. He believes that without education, you come out of prison the same age you entered. However, he admits that he participated in other programming only because it got him out of his cell block.

Once released from prison, Tony never looked back. He has not recidivated. He received no assistance from the state with reentry (job, housing, identification). He believes case workers are not especially interested in the success of inmates. He has not used any skills or training that he received while incarcerated, though he has benefited from his anger management classes. When he was released, he had no driver's license and no experience with cell phones, laptops, or social media. He worked briefly as a dishwasher but has worked for most of the time since he was released as a plumber. He has not experienced difficulty finding a job due to his criminal record. He has done what he promised himself he would do; that is, start a family. He is happily married and has a wife, a seven-year-old daughter, and a stepdaughter. He does not trust or make friends easily, and he does not wish to be around bad influences. He keeps to himself and does what he should, just as he did in prison.

Tony's philosophy is very simple. He got himself in trouble and worked his own way through it and out again. He does not blame the system or his youth for his prison time. He does not believe in a victim mentality. He believes in taking personal responsibility for one's own actions (this is reminiscent of behavioral cognitive therapy). He believes that successful reintegration is up to individual desire and he does not believe that institutional programming makes a big difference. He feels that many inmates are not truly interested in programs, but only participate to have something to do to fill their time. They are working the system. Inmates must learn to hate prison, unlike those who adapt to the environment and feel at home, if they are going to keep from coming back.

Tony would advise those coming out of prisons to rely on themselves and work hard. It takes a strong mind and applying your skills to be successful. Success is available, and mistakes from the past do not limit that possibility. Those who have never been inside but wish to help cannot understand the experiences of former inmates. Peer mentors can be a great help because they do understand (and can provide social capital). Getting employment is important, and former inmates are great workers as they will do anything for $7.25 an hour, when they were earning $0.40 per hour while incarcerated. Tony is glad that the author of this book was able to talk with someone who experienced it.

CONCLUSION

Recidivism is a huge problem in the United States. Overcrowded prisons are a drain on financial resources and are impacting entire communities. The cost of recidivism is devastating to future victims. The problem must be addressed, but the willingness and ability of our societal and criminal justice system to deal with the issue is clearly inadequate. Our current penal system does not do nearly enough to meet the needs of people reentering society after incarceration. The cycle must be broken.

As the information in this book has shown, recidivism is not a completely unsolvable problem. Our society, both inside and outside of prison, can provide the means and tools to deal with recidivism. Research proves that there are effective interventions. Education programs reduce recidivism. Successful employment helps prevent future incarceration. Substance abuse rehabilitation and mental health programming (including cognitive behavioral therapy) assist with the return to society. Reentry programs reduce the return to prison. Faith-based programs provide needed inspiration and support to prevent future offending. Social capital and practical assistance give former offenders skills and tools to prevent future offending and the return to prison.

The author's hope for this book is that it will be a call to action and a push to think of prison and reentry differently. We must provide needed resources to returning citizens including education, employment, rehabilitation treatment, reentry programming, faith-based programs, and social capital. If these resources are not offered, there is no reason to doubt that former offenders will return to their old criminal behaviors. We must put more of our efforts and resources toward alleviating these issues. In the end, we will save money spent on criminal justice and prisons. We will create healthy, economically productive people. We will save lives, injuries, and property from future crime. We will be a safer, more stable society. Not all who are convicted of a crime are equally capable of rehabilitation, but the necessary mechanisms must be made available for those who are willing and able to work toward success. Everyone in our nation will benefit from this important investment, and all involved deserve the effort. Let's all work together to do this.

Conclusion

This book has laid out all the research to show that prison programming has a positive statistical effect on reducing recidivism. There are strong arguments to be made, to be sure. However, it is important to get a more qualitative view of how inmates are impacted. The following is an interview with a participant in Campbell University's Sampson Correctional Program. He was ultimately dismissed from the program for a disciplinary issue. The questions explore prison programming and its impact on him. In order that his voice not be lost, I have included his responses exactly as they were given. Because of the opportunities he was given, he has hope for the future.

"Name All the Types of Programming That You Have Received While Incarcerated."

During my incarceration I've been located at 10 separate institutions; however, the majority of my incarceration was spent at Bertie Correctional closed custody (four and a half years) at Sampson Correctional medium custody (three years). As far as faith-based programs go, aside from regular worship services, I have experienced none. Not because of a lack of interest, my Christian faith played a huge part in my upbringing, there just isn't any that's been provided where I have been located. I have attended worship services, yet no programs. The COVID-19 pandemic did away with worship services for a while and then from what I've experienced, Christian services here put on a back burner to make way for other faith-based services.

Counseling/Therapy: This here I have experienced by choice. Honestly there isn't really any of this provided. Now don't get me wrong, if you need it you're able to sign up medically to see a mental health professional. I often have experienced depression and anxiety, for which at two separate times I've signed up to see a professional. These two individuals provided two drastically different approaches when attempting to deal with my concerns. Truth be told, there is absolutely nothing wrong with prayer, but the older gentleman I saw in 2016–2017 thought the answer to every one of my plights was prayer. Prayer does achieve tremendous feats, although help to assist the prayer's fruition is at times needed as well. Not a good experience.

In my second experience earlier in the year was a much different and better one. I actually felt that the woman was listening and actively trying to identify strategies that would assist me with my struggles. I left the sessions feeling like weight had been removed from my shoulders.

Educational Programming: Once at Pamlico Correctional, at then twice on my own. I've noticed throughout the duration of my incarceration that, aside from GED, there aren't many educational opportunities provided. Really it's more of vocational training, attempting to affix you with a certain "trait" that you'll be able to shop around upon release. OK at Pamlico Correctional I enrolled in this HST program they had started and I finished two classes they offered via a local community college, Counseling 125 and Interview Techniques. Then on my own I contacted UNC Chapel Hill and have taken two courses from them through the Bill and Ida Friday Center. They were self-paced, Communication 120 and American History from 1865 until now (2020). I completed the Comm 120 and due to Text Behind and my relocation from Sampson Correctional, I wasn't able to turn in the remainder of my assignments and schedule my exam (final).

Then finally, back in 2017 through my mother's assistance, I contacted Blackstone Career Institute and took a one and a half year Paralegal course through them that I completed in mid-2020, while I was partaking in the Campbell program, it was a self-based course with a two year time limit that I had to pay for.

Training: I have taken an HVAC course, Commercial Cleaning course (at two separate facilities) and then Career Readiness twice as well, they teach you, like, how to make a resume and go through the interview process, etc.

"What Did You Gain from Programs You Participated In?"

From my counseling/therapy services in 2016–2017, I gained nothing except for the feeling that I'd never be able to receive the assistance that I needed, I believe the gentleman's methods weren't "professional" and only saw me as some inmate trying to get one over on the state. I'd often try to engage from meaningful dialogue about my situation with my son and his mother and I was just met by some of the most ineffective assistance I've ever experienced.

From my experience earlier in this year I was provided strategies to utilize in assisting myself through my struggles. I felt engaged by the psychologist and could tell she knew what she was doing because of having taken three psychology courses through Campbell, many things she'd offer were reaffirmed by my prior knowledge.

From the Training/Vocational programs: I must be truthful, I learned how to properly sanitize various areas and how to strip, seal, wax and buff a floor from my Commercial Cleaning course at Bertie Correctional, and to never mix Clorox and Windex!! This is because I felt like these would be good things to know in everyday life moving forward, not because I'd seek this sort of employment.

The HVAC course that I took was continuing ed so there was an assumption you had some prior knowledge of HVAC systems, I was 21 and just got to prison, I knew nothing. But it was like all a "sham," it didn't matter because all he [the instructor] did was watch movies, of various genres, and leave early almost daily and on test days they were open book. It was like a shell corporation or like a "paper course," I felt highly disappointed. I knew less leaving than going in.

My second trip at Commercial Cleaning was the same as the HVAC, a "paper course," I mean *seriously* we literally used "text books" from 2004, in 2022. The teacher would offer bits and pieces from his personal experience, but then we were left to our own devices for the remainder, often to watch him sleep. I often left feeling disrespected for many reasons, like among many "you're cheating taxpayer dollars, for coming in sleeping and not teaching." I often felt degraded by even sitting through such, so I removed myself from that course, I was at Columbus Correctional for that one.

Honestly what I've noticed for the 10 years of my incarceration is that this is a commonality amongst institutions. There is some course with some "teacher" having been at that facility for an external time, this teacher has become so conditioned by the Institutional setting themselves that they begin to act as a correctional officer rather than a "teacher." The case managers we're provided spearhead individuals into these programs, funded by the state, many don't want anything to do with the program itself, they only do it to get the "gain days" you're provided each month. This breeds a toxic environment; you may even have a monthly teacher wanting to teach, but after constantly facing a "class" un-wanting and un-willing to learn, they become fixated in "the process." Meaning they get paid whether we learn, finish or not. So they lose their energy and will, which leaves those of us wanting to learn on the short end. You still have the course books, so you can read yourself, yet there's next to no instruction, and this is a strong commonality amongst these vocational programs around the state.

On the educational program side, I gained a strong deal from my Comm 120 and American History 1865–Today course and my Paralegal diploma course. In Comm 120 I gained the importance of interpersonal relationships and how diversified backgrounds and experiences shape our interactions within these relationships. I often use many of the skills expressed, like active listening, open-minded questions, not too many I statements. . . . When I'd turn in assignments there was a section for any question posed, and upon response of my grades, thoughtful and well-devised answers would be provided to many questions. In my American History course I gained a more insightful look into our history as a nation and was provided a more adept and in-depth look and explanation of Restoration, the Radical Republicans, and how the transcontinental railroad really came to bring our nation together. These two courses were offered through UNC-Chapel Hill.

My paralegal course added to my personal foundation by reiterating the morals and principals that I was raised on. Thus guiding the remainder of my future. It really strengthened my admiration and love for our founding fathers and what our great nation is founded upon, inalienable rights. I was provided an overview of the history of our law system and some major turning points in the history of law, such as the Magna Carta. Then I gained better understanding of the various types of law from civil to criminal, to wills, trust, torts, contracts and corporations. Within each of these I was provided a history and great explanation; what I found the hardest was property law.

Finally, from Counseling 125 and Interview techniques I gained a lot, each of which was backed up further in my Comm 120 and psychology and sociology classes. However, this setup for these courses at Pamlico was horrible, like with Campbell we had 4 courses a week one on each day, at Pamlico we had one course daily for like a month to one and a half months, it was difficult to actually learn anything, so I'd keep my books and make detailed notes that I'd study over for months, taking as much away as possible from the text.

As far as worship services go, they continue to ground me and provide the much needed calming and guidance required for me to lead a healthy, positive and very productive life now and upon my re-entry into society.

"What Did You Gain from Your Campbell Education?"

First and foremost this journey is near and dear to my heart, I mean for 24 months, through COVID-19, I lived, breathed, slept, and ate with my text books, lessons, and instruction. It became a part of me and forever a piece of who I am. While many looked at the recognition one gains from having Campbell on your "degree," I understand that the actual "degree" is the knowledge that is transferred from your instructors to you and the "paper" degree is symbolic of your ability to have successfully retained and apply that knowledge. I gained a tremendous education that I'm proud of, proud to speak of and share and formed relationships that have forever changed my life for the better. My eyes and mind were opened to a whole new way of life. The knowledge I've gained allows me to formulate thought in previously unimagined ways, giving me hope for the future for me and my son. I was given high-quality teachers throughout every course, more than exceeding my expectation held with credentials too numerous to list. Just having been taught by who taught me provided me with extra drive to get the best out of me and the most out of my education. I'm forever grateful to Campbell University and each and every one of the professors that that transferred knowledge from their well to my cup. So much emphasis and focus was placed on critical thinking and a growth mindset, I almost "fact check" everything and preach constantly to my 14-year-old, just started high school, to be receptive to new information, factual of course, even when it challenges your already held beliefs and thoughts. This was major for me and a challenge, which I love, to have the ability to challenge your beliefs with truth that serves them as false and change them is a tremendous stride that I made. I learned so much from being able to recognize cognitive biases, such as belief perseverance, that I consciously analyze my thought when providing thought or opinion to a process. I even became able to recognize how we learn and "forget" as humans, such as with the recency and primacy effects, that when I study I'm aware of where my deficiency comes from, so I pay even more attention in those areas. Overall I gained much-needed resources, information, skills, abilities, and the self-confidence I need to become a positive and productive contributory citizen upon my release.

"Why Did You Choose the Programs That You Did?"

When I first came to prison 10 years ago I was 21, I was so overwhelmed with the 15–21 year sentence I was just beginning. I knew I needed something to keep busy with and learning was a strong point. This is what led me to the HVAC course, yet upon arrival as I've stated previously [it] was a disappointment because I figured if I could gain a general understanding there'd eventually be money to be made in that field. My attempt at HVAC was to gain the needed information integral to that skill set because I thought initially physical labor would be my only option upon release.

With the Commercial Cleaning courses, I looked at them as a way to gain a "better" job within the institution, for upon the completion you immediately receive a job allowing more access to the facility and extended time out of your cell to complete your job assignment. This was big in closed custody where you may be locked in the cell for over 24 hours repeatedly. I grew more discouraged because growing up I was always taught to believe in the system because it works, it isn't biased, the people who run it are who control it. But I began to feel and know I failed the system by coming to prison, but I'm here now trying to correct myself and the system is failing me.

I didn't take any course for over four years until 2017. I began to self-assess and take a deep meaningful look at myself in the mirror, then I knew I'm thirsty for knowledge, I want to learn and I won't be relegated to physical labor. So as I spoke with an acquaintance he introduced me to the paralegal course via correspondence. I immediately contacted my family who was more than willing to assist with the financial side, and signed up.

My drive and yearning for knowledge drove me to the paralegal course. I know with my record that field may not be a choice, however, it doesn't prevent me from gaining the knowledge and using it later, and it creates more versatility and opens other avenues for me.

Once I got my mind churning again it became an unquenchable thirst, I began to research for more educational opportunities even if I had to pay for them. This led to my networking in various circles of others exemplifying the same desire for learning as myself. In doing so, I found out about the Bill and Ida Friday Center at UNC-Chapel Hill and the fact that they offer self-paced correspondence courses, so I signed up for Comm 120 first because I knew communication also creates versatility and opportunities. I began my journey for educational growth.

On this journey, and while taking both my paralegal course and Comm 120, I was transferred to Sampson and found out about the Upstart program from Campbell University. I knew of the school already, I mean who from NC doesn't know of Campbell, right, and they had offered my brother a wrestling scholarship in 2017, he chose to follow his girlfriend to Methodist. I didn't hesitate and was one of the original signees for the program in 2019. I mean the name Campbell University draws a certain degree of respect, integrity, and dignity, so I went in with certain expectations from the program. In my first year I was taking four courses and my two separate courses and managed to make the President's list at Campbell, finish the Paralegal course with a 98 average and complete Comm 120 with an A in the class and a B on the 350-question final. I see that my will and want for something better for myself drew me to the educational programs that I chose, having all meant something close and personal to me.

"Do Prison Programs Improve an Inmate's Chances of Success?"

Yes, I know that they've drastically improved mine. Where does success begin though? Is it in the program or the person? I believe it's in the desire of the person and the program becomes an assistive measure. A person can take a million courses and programs, passing them all, and choose to do nothing with the information and skills they possess. The individual has to possess the will, the want, and the driving desire to overcome their incarceration and provide a better life for themselves, if these are possessed, then the adequate programs can and will aid in the individual's chances of success. As before, the more you're able to retain and apply creates versatility and shows another the time and effort you've put into your personal ability. It shows your desire, thus creating a thought in another about providing an opportunity. In the system, individuals with this want can get lost in the "paper courses" offering no real discourse, the program has to fulfill its role as assistant. The universe has to align properly, it has to be the right facility, the right warden, the right prison programmers, the right individuals (inmates) and the right program with instructors provided. There must be a general overall consensus of success, desire, and drive like we had with Campbell at Sampson. The warden was a Campbell grad, the program was a way to give back, the facility was medium custody and the nicest I've been to, as far as laid-back-wise, you had 11 people with a desire to attain success, and professors from Campbell never have been in this setting with a yearning to teach and relay information. They didn't know the prison way, they knew the Campbell way. I know my educational success was important when Dr. Truffin came in one day and said, "I've been teaching you for a while now and call you Mr. whomever,. but what do want to be called?" With that, I knew I was looked at as a person and ensuring I gained the necessary information to be successful was all that mattered. You know, it was a running inside joke I made once: "we're not in prison going to college, we're in college having to sleep in prison." Campbell was my getaway where my aspirations and dreams were still able to live and thrive.

"Why Would You Say You Were Not Successful in Completing the Bachelor's Degree from Campbell?"

Well this is a tough one and something I've been dealing with for the last 15 months I've been gone. It, well first let me say, although after only one month into it I was removed, I did complete my Associate's degree with a 4.0 GPA, made the President's list every semester for A honors, and garnered election into the Sigma Gamma Chapter of Alpha Sigma Lambda at Campbell University, lifetime membership. Three feats not easily attained. My intellectual ability wasn't the factor; when signing up for the program, the contract, there was no mention of infractions. Well five months into the program several individuals caught infractions, several were removed from the program. We expressed our dismay, so they added a "memo" saying some infractions would be addressed, yet only "A" class infractions constitute removal. In here there are A, B, and C class infractions, A being the highest classification. Well in September 2021, me and another individual has a disagreement, he was in the beginning Associates program. We both got into this situation that sadly resulted in us both getting a "B" class infraction. Five days later the other gentleman was allowed to return, they didn't allow for my return, no explanation, nothing. He stayed, I left. I'd have to say that I was unsuccessful because at a single moment I let emotions get the best of me, being unable to outwit another and walk away. I was therefore removed for my infraction. I loved and still love the school and program so much that it's been hard for me, although it lives with me forever! I had the time of my life with Campbell and my professors, for that I'm forever grateful. Since then my pride has been an area that I've been working on since I see it as a deficiency when it begins to cloud judgement, another reason I sought counseling services earlier this year. I'm making strides, step by step.

"What Are Your Goals When You Are Released?"

I want to refresh and strengthen my relationship with my son, I left when he was four and will return when he's 19. He just began high school in August, our relationship has consistence in the communication department, and it's just hard on us both with me not being physically present. I've now also been on the receiving end of a tremendous blessing via my education, which has inspired me to pay it forward and seek to give back to the community. I also am a firm believer in mental health awareness. This past year and a half, I've been learning (attempting to) the ins and outs of a non-profit. I'm going to begin my own, I want to raise mental health awareness and coordinate resources, eventually hoping to offer them. Under my organization I also want to assist the youth, men and women, on the wrong way prior to being incarcerated through educational and faith services as their mentorship. Also while addressing the recidivism rate, I'll actively assist them through similar means and aid these to truly want the change necessary for success in their life. I'll surround myself with a good team and resources. I want to partner with other entities in doing so until hopefully I'm able to sustain everything from within. I want to fulfil the mission of the school and give back to the community through active service, making a change in the life of others by giving them meaningful opportunities. I will assist adolescents and adult offenders, women and men, and advocacy.

References

Allen, L. C., MacKenzie, D. L., and Hickman, L. J. (2001). The effectiveness of cognitive behavioral treatment for adult offenders: A methodological, quality-based review. *International Journal of Offender Therapy 45*(4). https://journals.sagepub.com/doi/pdf/10.1177/0306624X01454009.

Andrews, D. A., Zinger, R. D., Bonta, J., Gendreau, P., and Cullen, F. T. (1990). *Does correctional treatment work? A clinically relevant and psychologically informed meta-analysis*. Office of Justice Programs. https://www.ojp.gov/ncjrs/virtual-library/abstracts/does-correctional-treatment-work-clinically-relevant-and.

Aos, S., Phipps, P., Barnoski, R., and Lieb, R. (2018). The costs and benefits of programs to reduce crime. *Washington State Institute for Public Policy*, 149–75. DOI: 10.4324/9780429501265-6.

Arbour, W., Lacroix, G., and Marchand, S. (2021). Prison rehabilitation programs: Efficiency and targeting. Retrieved March 23, 2023, from https://www3.cirano.qc.ca/files/publications/2021s-01.pdf.

Associated Press. (2017, June 4). At $75,560, housing a prisoner in California now costs more than a year at Harvard. *Los Angeles Times*. http://www.latimes.com/local/lanow/la-me-prison-costs-20170604-htmlstory.html#.

Aukerman, M. J. (2003). Barriers to reentry: Legal strategies to reduce recidivism and promote the success of ex-offenders. *Michigan Criminal Law Annual Journal, 1*(1), 1–56. http://higherlogicdownload.s3.amazonaws.com/MICHBAR/fc62ec40-d5df-49b4-a153-adc2eecb7c39/UploadedImages/pdfs/CLAnnual04.pdf#page=4.

Baladi, R. (2017, October 31). Defy ventures: Investing in the future at Pelican Bay state prison. *Smart Recruiters*. https://www.smartrecruiters.com/blog/defy-ventures-investing-in-the-future-at-pelican-bay-state-prison/.

Benecchi, L. (2021, August 8). Recidivism imprisons American Progress. *Harvard Political Review*. https://harvardpolitics.com/recidivism-american-progress/.

Boyd, A. (n.d.). Rehabilitation programs division. Retrieved April 21, 2021, from https://www.tdcj.texas.gov/divisions/rpd/inner_change.html.

Bridges to Life (n.d.). History and mission. Retrieved April 21, 2021, from http://www.bridgestolife.org/index.php?option=com_content&view=article&id=3&Itemid=62.

Bright, L. C., and Graham, M. G. (n.d.). Faith-based programs give facilities a helping hand. U.S. Department of Justice. Retrieved April 11, 2021, from https://www.ojp.gov/pdffiles1/nij/221896.pdf.

Buck, G. (2018). The core conditions of peer mentoring. *Criminology & Criminal Justice, 18*(2), 190–206. https://doi.org/10.1177/1748895817699659.

Bureau of Prisons, Justice. (2016). *Annual determination of average cost of incarceration, 81*). Washington, DC: Office of Federal Register.

Bureau of Prisons. (2018). Annual Determination of Average Cost of Incarceration. *The Federal Register, 83*(83), 18863-18863.

Center for Employment Opportunities. (n.d.). About us. Retreived March 7, 2023, from https://ceoworks.org/.

Center for Immigration Studies. (2018, May 21). *A brief examination of the First Step Act: Immigration concerns with the Criminal Justice Reform Bill.* https://cis.org/Report/Brief-Examination-FIRST-STEP-Act.

Chandler, R., Fletcher, B., and Volkow, N. (2009). Treating drug abuse and addiction in the criminal justice system: Improving public health and safety. *JAMA, 301*(2), 183–90. https://doi.org/10.1001/jama.2008.976.

Christian Library International (n.d.). Vision. Retrieved March 7, 2023, from http://cli.world/about-4/statement-of-faith/.

CoreCivic. (2018, April). *The recidivism problem.* https://www.corecivic.com/hubfs/_brand_resources/_factsheets/FACTSHEET-Reentry-Commitment-DRAFT1.pdf.

Council of State Governments Justice Center. (2020, March 5). Second Chance Act Grant Program. https://csgjusticecenter.org/publications/second-chance-act/.

Crime in America. (2021, July 29). *Federal research: Long prison sentences significantly reduce crime and recidivism.* https://www.crimeinamerica.net/federal-research-long-prison-sentences-significantly-reduce-crime-and-recidivism/.

Cullen, F. T., and Gendreau, P. (1989). The effectiveness of correctional rehabilitation: Reconsidering the "nothing works" debate. In L. Goodstein and D. L. MacKenzie (Eds.), *The American prison: Issues in research and policy* (pp. 23–44). Plenum Press.

Cullen, F., and Gendreau, P. (2001). From nothing works to what works: Changing professional ideology in the 21st century. *The Prison Journal, 81*(3), 313–38. https://doi.org/10.1177/0032885501081003002.

D'Abruzzo, D., and Chapman, C. (2016). Vera Institute of Justice. https://www.vera.org/.

Daley, M., Love, C. T., Shepard, D. S., Petersen, C. B., White, K. L., and Hall, F. B. (2004). Cost-effectiveness of Connecticut's in-prison substance abuse treatment. *Journal of Offender Rehabilitation, 39*, 69–92. https://doi.org/10.1300/J076v39n03_04.

Davis, L., Bozick, R., Steele, J., Saunders, J., and Miles, J. (2013). *Evaluating the effectiveness of correctional education: A meta-analysis of programs that provide education to incarcerated adults.* RAND Corporation. https://www.rand.org/pubs/research_reports/RR266.html.

Davis, L., Steele, J., Bozick, R., Williams, M., Turner, S., Miles, J., Saunders, J., and Steinberg, P. (2014). *How effective is correctional education, and where do we go from here? The results of a comprehensive evaluation*. RAND Corporation. https://www.rand.org/pubs/research_reports/RR564.html.

De Claire, K., and Dixon, L. (2017). The effects of prison visits from family members on prisoners' well-being, prison rule breaking, and recidivism: A review of research since 1991. *Trauma, Violence, & Abuse, 18*(2), 185–99. https://doi.org/10.1177/1524838015603209.

Denver, Siwach, G., and Bushway, S. D. (2017). A new look at the employment and recidivism relationship through the lens of a criminal background check. *Criminology* (Beverly Hills), *55*(1), 174–204. https://doi.org/10.1111/1745–9125.12130.

Dodson, K. D., Cabage, L. N., and Klenowski, P. M. (2011, August). An evidence-based assessment of faith-based programs: Do faith-based programs "work" to reduce recidivism. *Journal of Offender Rehabilitation 50*(6):367-383. https://www.researchgate.net/publication/232992536_An_Evidence-Based_Assessment_of_Faith-Based_Programs_Do_Faith-Based_Programs_Work_to_Reduce_Recidivism.

Dumville, R., and Hunt, K. (2016). *Recidivism among federal offenders: A comprehensive overview*. Washington, DC: United States Sentencing Commission.

Duwe, G., and Johnson, B. R. (2013). Estimating the benefits of a faith-based correctional program. *International Journal of Criminology and Sociology 2*, 227–39. http://www.baylorisr.org/wp-content/uploads/benefits_faith-based_correctional_program.pdf.

Farley, H., and Pike, A. (2016). Engaging prisoners in education: Reducing risk and recidivism. *Advancing Corrections: Journal of the International Corrections and Prisons Association, 1*, 65–73.

Fazel, S., Bains, P., and Doll, H. (2006, February), Substance abuse and dependence in prisoners: a systematic review. *Addiction, 101,* 181–91. doi:10.1111/j.1360-0443.2006.01316.x.

Federal Bureau of Investigation. (2015). *Uniform crime report: Crime in the United States, 2014.* https://ucr.fbi.gov/crime-in-the-u.s/2014/crime-in-the-u.s.-2014/offenses-known-to-law-enforcement/violent crime/violent-crime.

Federal Bureau of Prisons. (2017, March 6). Prison reform: Reducing recidivism by strengthening the Federal Bureau of Prisons. U.S. Department of Justice. https://www.justice.gov/archives/prison-reform.

Flavin, J. (2004, March 7). *Employment counseling, housing assistance . . . and aunt Yolanda?: How strengthening families' social capital can reduce recidivism. Criminology and Public Policy 3*(2). https://onlinelibrary.wiley.com/doi/10.1111/j.1745–9133.2004.tb00036.x.

Full Circle Fund. (2020). The last mile/defy ventures. https://www.fullcirclefund.org/single-post/2017/09/01/The-Last-Mile-Defy-Ventures.

Gaynes, E. (2005, January 10). Prisoner Reentry: Helping Former Prisoners Return to Communities. Retrieved March 23, 2023, from https://assets.aecf.org/m/resourcedoc/aecf-ReentryHelpingFormerPrisoners-2005.pdf.

Gill, C., and Wilson, D. B. (2016). Improving the success of reentry programs. *Criminal Justice and Behavior*, *44*(3), 336–59. https://doi.org/10.1177/0093854816682048.

Global Justice Resource Center. (n.d.). About Us. Retrieved November 4, 2022, from https://globaljusticerc.org/about-us/#who-we-are.

Goldstein, E. H., Warner-Robbins, C., McClean, C., Macatula, L., and Conklin, R. (2009). A peer-driven mentoring case management community reentry model: An application for jails and prisons. *Family & Community Health, 32*(4), 309–13. https://doi.org/10.1097/FCH.0b013e3181b91f0d.

Guevara, M., and Solomon, E. (2009, October). Implementing evidence-based practice in community corrections. Retrieved March 23, 2023, from https://www.crj.org/assets/2017/07/Community_Corrections_BoxSet_Oct09.pdf.

Harrison, L. (2001). The revolving prison door for drug-involved offenders: Challenges and opportunities. *Crime and Delinquency*, *47*(3), 462–84. https://doi.org/10.1177/0011128701047003010.

Hartman, M. (2021, June). Ban the box policy snapshot. Retrieved March 23, 2023, from https://documents.ncsl.org/wwwncsl/Criminal-Justice/Ban-the-Box-Policy-Snapshot.pdf.

Haven House Services (n.d.). *Mission & History*. https://www.havenhousenc.org/about/mission-history/.

Head, T., and DeRoche, C. (2017, January 29). How faith can curb recidivism. *The Hill*. https://thehill.com/blogs/pundits-blog/crime/316780-how-faith-can-curb-recidivism/.

Henrichson, C., Schattner-Elmaleh, E., Kang-Brown, J., Hinds, O., and Wallace-Lee, J. (2019, December). Incarceration trends in Texas - Vera Institute of Justice. Retrieved March 23, 2023, from https://www.vera.org/downloads/pdfdownloads/state-incarceration-trends-texas.pdf.

Hiller, M., Knight, K., and Simpson, D. (1999). Prison-based substance abuse treatment, residential aftercare and recidivism. *Addiction (Abingdon, England)*, *94*(6), 833–42. https://doi.org/10.1046/j.1360–0443.1999.9468337.x.

Hooper, R. M., Lockwood, D., and Inciardi, J. A. (1993). Treatment techniques in corrections-based therapeutic communities. *The Prison Journal*, *73*(3), 290–306. https://doi.org/10.1177/0032855593073003004.

Howell, R. (2013). Criminal justice initiatives. Retrieved 2023, from https://www.ptrc.org/home/showpublisheddocument/3082/636573374393630000.

Hudson Link for Higher Education in Prison. (2022, October 25). Impact. https://hudsonlink.org/.

Hughes, T., and Wilson, D. (2004). Reentry trends in the United States. Bureau of Justice Statistics. Retrieved December 1, 2022, from https://bjs.ojp.gov/content/pub/pdf/reentry.pdf.

James, D. (2004). Profile of jail inmates, 2002. NCJ 201932. Washington, DC: U.S Department of Justice, Bureau of Justice Statistics.

James, N. (2015). Offender Reentry: Correctional statistics, reintegration into the community, and recidivism. Congressional Research Service. https://sgp.fas.org/crs/misc/RL34287.pdf.

Johnson, B. (2004). Religious programs and recidivism among former inmates in Prison Fellowship programs: A long-term follow-up study. *Justice Quarterly, 21*(2), 329354. https://doi.org/10.1080/07418820400095831.

Jonson, and Cullen, F. T. (2015). Prisoner reentry programs. *Crime & Justice (Chicago, Ill), 44*(1), 517–75. https://doi.org/10.1086/681554.

Kelly, C., Welsh, W., and Stanley, J. (2019). The treatment group and recidivism: A multilevel analysis of prison-based substance abuse treatment. *Prison Journal*, *99*(5), 515–34. https://doi.org/10.1177/0032885519875002.

Knight, K., Simpson, D. D., and Hiller, M. L. (1999). Three-year reincarceration outcomes for in-prison therapeutic community treatment in Texas. *The Prison Journal*, *79*(3), 337–51. https://doi.org/10.1177/0032885599079003004.

Latessa, E., Cullen, F., and Listwan, S. (2006, December). How to prevent prisoner re-entry programs from failing: Insights from evidence-based corrections. Retrieved March 23, 2023, from https://www.uc.edu/content/dam/uc/ics/docs/ListwanCullenLatessaHowToPrevent.pdf.

Latessa, E. J., Sperber, K. G., and Makarios, M. D. (2013, July 9). *Establishing a risk-dosage research agenda: Implications for policy and practice. Justice Research and Policy 15*(1). https://journals.sagepub.com/doi/pdf/10.3818/JRP.15.1.2013.123.

Lattimore, P. K., and Visher, C. A. (2014). The impact of prison reentry services on short-term outcomes. *Evaluation Review*, *37*(3–4), 274–313. https://doi.org/10.1177/0193841x13519105.

La Vigne, N., Davies, E., Palmer, T., and Haalberstadt, R. (2008, September). Release planning for successful reentry. Urban Institute. https://www.urban.org/sites/default/files/publication/32056/411767-Release-Planning-for-Successful-Reentry.PDF.

Lester, D., and Van Voorhis, P. (1997). Psychoanalytic therapy. In Van Voorhis et al., *Correctional Counseling and Rehabilitation* (Third Edition), 109–25. https://www.ojp.gov/ncjrs/virtual-library/abstracts/psychoanalytic-therapy-correctional-counseling-and-rehabilitation.

Liggett, B. (2022, November 23). "Adversity into action": Second Chance Initiative expands to women's re-entry program. *Campbell University News*. https://news.campbell.edu/articles/adversity-into-action-second-chance-initiative-expands-to-womens-re-entry-program/?fbclid=IwAR0M-9ddNs8gEhiPDsf1G6PlyGzb15jDap5ROnwQEVBfnv22PT39AQIL2Qo.

Lockwood, B., and Lewis, N. (2019). The hidden cost of incarceration. The Marshall Project. https://www.themarshallproject.org/2019/12/17/the-hidden-cost-of-incarceration.

Madrigal, A. C. (2018, October 19). Big tech's newest experiment in criminal justice reform. The Atlantic Monthly. https://www.theatlantic.com/technology/archive/2018/08/big-techs-newest-experiment-in-criminal-justice-reform/568849/.

Makarios, M., Steiner, B., and Travis, L. F. (2010). III Examining the predictors of recidivism among men and women released from prison in Ohio. Criminal Justice and Behavior. *37,* 1377–1391.

Mallik-Kane, K., and Visher, C. A. (2008). *Health and prisoner reentry: How physical, mental, and substance abuse conditions shape the process of reintegration* (p. 82). Washington, DC: Urban Institute Justice Policy Center.

Mark, Y., Gartner, J., O'Connor, T., Larson, D., and Wright, K. (1995). Long-term Recidivism Among Federal Inmates Trained as Volunteer Prison Ministers. *Journal of Offender Rehabilitation, 22*, 97–118. doi:10.1300/J076v22n01_07.

Marlow, E., Grajeda, W., Lee, Y., Young, E., Williams, M., and Hill, K. (2015). Peer Mentoring for Male Parolees: A CBPR Pilot Study. *Progress in Community Health Partnerships: Research, Education, and Action, 9*(1), 91–100. doi:10.1353/cpr.2015.0013.

Martin, S., Butzin, C., Saum, C., and Inciardi, J. (1999). Three-year outcomes of therapeutic community treatment for drug-involved offenders in Delaware: From prison to work release to aftercare. *The Prison Journal*, *79*(3), 294–320. https://doi.org/10.1177/0032885599079003002.

Martinson, R. (1974). What works? Questions and answers about prison reform. *The Public Interest*, *35*, 22–54.

Matthews, E. (2021). Peer-focused prison reentry programs: Which peer characteristics matter most? *Incarceration*. https://doi.org/10.1177/26326663211019958,

McCollister, K. E., and French, M. T. *The economic cost of substance abuse treatment in criminal justice settings.* Health Services Research Center and Department of Epidemiology and Public Health.

McCollister, K., French, M., Inciardi, J., Butzin, C., Martin, S., and Hooper, R. (2003). Post-release substance abuse treatment for criminal offenders: A cost-effectiveness analysis. *Journal of Quantitative Criminology*, *19*(4), 389–407. https://doi.org/10.1023/B:JOQC.0000005441.49529.61.

McCollister, K., French, M., Prendergast, M., Wexler, H., Sacks, S., and Hall, E. (2003). Is in-prison treatment enough? A cost-effectiveness analysis of prison-based treatment and aftercare services for substance-abusing offenders. *Law & Policy*, *25*(1), 63–82. https://doi.org/10.1111/1467–9930.00140.

Mears, D. P., Roman, C. G., Wolff, A., and Buck, J. (2006). Faith-based efforts to improve prisoner reentry: Assessing the logic and evidence. Prison Legal News. https://www.prisonlegalnews.org/media/publications/faith%20based%20rehabilitation%20efforts-journal%20of%20criminal%20justice-2006.pdf.

Morani, N. M., Wikoff, N., Linhorst, D. M., and Bratton, S. (2011). A description of the self-identified needs, service expenditures, and social outcomes of participants of a prisoner-reentry program. *The Prison Journal (Philadelphia, Pa.), 91*(3), 347–65. https://doi.org/10.1177/0032885511409896.

Mumola, C. J. (1999, January 5). *Substance abuse and treatment of state and federal prisoners, 1997.* Bureau of Justice Statistics. https://www.bjs.gov/index.cfm?ty=pbdetail&iid=1169.

Muresianu, A. (2018). Criminal justice reform is also good economics. Foundation for Economic Education. https://fee.org/articles/criminal-justice-reform-is-also-good-economics/.

Nally, John M., Lockwood, Susan, and Knutson, Katie. (2014). Post-release recidivism and employment among different types of released offenders: A 5-year follow-up study in the United States. *International Journal of Criminal Justice Sciences*, 9(1), 16–34.

National Conference of State Legislatures. (2023). Report connecting recently released prisoners to health care-how to leverage Medicaid. Retrieved March 24, 2023, from https://www.ncsl.org/civil-and-criminal-justice/connecting-recently-released-prisoners-to-health-carehow-to-leverage-medicaid.

National Institute of Justice. (2014). *Recidivism*. https://www.nij.gov/topics/corrections/recidivism/Pages/welcome.aspx.

National Reentry Resource Center. (2017, June). *Reducing recidivism: States deliver results*. https://csgjusticecenter.org/publications/reducing-recidivism-states-deliver-results-2017.

National Research Council. (2007). *Parole, desistance from crime, and community integration*. National Academies Press.

Nixon, S. (2020). "Giving back and getting on with my life": Peer mentoring, desistance and recovery of ex-offenders. *Probation Journal, 67*(1), 47–64. https://doi.org/10.1177/0264550519900249.

North Carolina adopts ban-the-box law. (2020, October 14). *National Crime Search Blog*. https://www.nationalcrimesearch.com/blog/north-carolina-adopts-ban-the-box-law/.

North Carolina Department of Public Safety. (2019). Cost of corrections. https://www.ncdps.gov/adult-corrections/cost-of-corrections.

O'Connor, T., Young, M. C., Gartner, J., Larson, D., M.D., and Wright, K. (2018, April 25). The impact of a volunteer prison ministry program on the long-term recidivism of federal inmates. Transforming Corrections. https://transformingcorrections.com/the-impact-of-a-volunteer-prison-ministry-program-on-the-long-term-recidivism-of-federal-inmates/.

Pager, D. (2006). Evidence-based policy for successful prisoner reentry. *Criminology and Public Policy* 5(3), 505–514https://onlinelibrary.wiley.com/doi/epdf/10.1111/j.1745–9133.2006.00391.x.

Peters, R. H., Greenbaum, P. E., Edens, J. F., Carter, C. R., and Ortiz, M. M. (1998). Prevalence of DSM-IV substance abuse and dependence disorders among prison inmates. *American Journal of Drug and Alcohol Abuse*, *24*(4), 573–87. https://doi.org/10.3109/00952999809019608.

Petersilia, J. (2003). *When prisoners return to the community: Political, economic, and social consequences* (No. 9). US Department of Justice, Office of Justice Programs, National Institute of Justice.

Petersilia, J. (2004). What Works in Prisoner Reentry?: Reviewing and Questioning the Evidence. *Federal Probation, 68*(2), 4–8. Retrieved March 23, 2023, from https://www.ojp.gov/ncjrs/virtual-library/abstracts/what-works-prisoner-reentry-reviewing-and-questioning-evidence.

Petersilia, J. (2011). Beyond the prison bubble. *The Wilson Quarterly*, *35*(1), 50–55. https://doi.org/10.1037/e725192011-005.

Petersilia J. (2014) Parole and prisoner reentry in the United States. In Bruinsma G., Weisburd D. (Eds), *Encyclopedia of Criminology and Criminal Justice*. Springer. https://doi.org/10.1007/978-1-4614-5690-2_22.

Pettus-Davis, C., Renn, T., Veeh, C., and Eikenberry, J. (2019). Intervention development study of the five-key model for reentry: An evidence-driven prisoner reentry intervention. *Journal of Offender Rehabilitation, 58*(7), 614–43. doi:10.1080/10509674.2019.1635242

Pogrebin, M., West-Smith, M., Walker, A., and Unnithan, N. P. (2014). Employment isn't enough. *Criminal Justice Review, 39*(4), 394–410. https://doi.org/10.1177/0734016814540303.

Prison College Program. (2021, November 15). Adams State University. https://www.adams.edu/academics/print-based/prison-college-program/.

Prison Fellowship. (n.d.). *Prison Fellowship Ministries*. https://www.prisonfellowship.org/.

Prison Policy Initiative. (n.d.). U.S. incarceration rates by race. Retrieved November 4, 2022, from https://www.prisonpolicy.org/graphs/raceinc.html.

Prison University Project.(2022, October 18). Mount Tamalpais College. https://www.mttamcollege.org/about/strategic-plan/.

Project Re-entry. (n.d.). *Project Re-Entry*. Retrieved November 4, 2022, from https://www.ptrc.org/services/criminal-justice/project-re-entry.

Reaching Out from Within. (n.d.). About: mission. Retrieved November 4, 2022, from https://www.rofw.org/mission-impact.

Reich, J. (2017, August 17). *The economic impact of prison rehabilitation programs.* Wharton School of Business. https://publicpolicy.wharton.upenn.edu/live/news/2059-the-economic-impact-of-prison-rehabilitation/for-students/blog/news.php.

Reingle Gonzalez, J. M., Rana, R. E., Jetelina, K. K., and Roberts, M. H. (2019). The value of lived experience with the criminal justice system: A qualitative study of peer re-entry specialists. *International Journal of Offender Therapy and Comparative Criminology, 63*(10), 1861–1875. https://doi.org/10.1177/0306624X19830596.

Rotman, E. (1990). Beyond Punishment: A New View on the Rehabilitation of Criminal Offenders. Greenwood Press.

Santora, M. (2013, August 23). City's annual cost per inmate is $168,000, study finds. *New York Times*. https://www.nytimes.com/2013/08/24/nyregion/citys-annual-cost-per-inmate-is-nearly-168000-study-says.html.

Seiter, R. P., and Kadela, K. R. (2003). Prisoner reentry: What works, what does not, and what is promising. *Crime and Delinquency, 49*(3), 360–88. https://doi.org/10.1177/0011128703049003002.

Sells, D., Curtis, A., Abdur-Raheem, J., Klimczak, M., Barber, C., Meaden, C., Hasson, J., Fallon, P., and Emigh-Guy, M. (2020). Peer-mentored community reentry reduces recidivism. *Criminal Justice and Behavior, 47*(4), 437–56. https://doi.org/10.1177/0093854820901562.

Serin, R. (2005, December). *Evidence-based practice: Framework for enhancing correctional results in prisons*. National Institute of Corrections. https://www.cjinstitute.org/assets/sites/2/2009/03/40e_Prison_BoxSet_Sep09.pdf.

Simmons, M. M., Fincke, B. G., Drainoni, M.-L., Kim, B., Byrne, T., Smelson, D., Casey, K., Ellison, M. L., Visher, C., Blue-Howells, J., and McInnes, D. K. (2017). A two-state comparative implementation of peer-support intervention to link veterans to health-related services after incarceration: A study protocol. *BMC Health Services Research, 17*(1), 647. https://doi.org/10.1186/s12913-017-2572-x.

Smith, E., and Hattery, A. (2011). Can social capital networks assist re-entry felons to overcome barriers to re-entry and reduce recidivism? *Sociation Today 9*(1). Retrieved September 29, 2021, from http://www.ncsociology.org/sociationtoday/v91/reentry.htm.

Stahler, G. J., Mennis, J., Belenko, S., Welsh, W. N., Hiller, M. L., and Zajac, G. (2013). Predicting recidivism for released state prison offenders: Examining the influence of individual and neighborhood characteristics and spatial contagion on the likelihood of reincarceration. *Criminal Justice and Behavior, 40*(6), 690–711.

StepUp Ministry (n.d.). Our motivation. Retrieved March 7, 2023, from https://www.stepupministry.org/who-we-are-1/

Sumrall, R., Sumrall, W., and Doss, D. (2016). A review of correctional philosophies toward reaffirming rehabilitation as an Ohio correctional paradigm. *International Journal of Business and Social Science*, *7*(5), 1–8.

The Bob Barker Foundation. (n.d.). *We're working to defeat recidivism.* https://www.bobbarkerfoundation.org/

The Sentencing Project. (2020). Criminal justice facts. https://www.sentencingproject.org/criminal-justice-facts/.

Travis, J. (2000, May). But they all come back: Rethinking prisoner reentry. U.S. Department of Justice. https://www.ojp.gov/pdffiles1/nij/181413.pdf.

Trusty, B., and Eisenberg, M. (2003, February). Initial process and outcome evaluation of the innerchange freedom initiative: The faith-based prison program in tdcj. Office of Justice Programs. https://www.ojp.gov/ncjrs/virtual-library/abstracts/initial-process-and-outcome-evaluation-innerchange-freedom.

Uria, D. (2018, May 22). House passes prison reform bill aimed at reducing recidivism. United Press International. https://www.upi.com/Top_News/US/2018/05/22/House-passes-prison-reform-bill-aimed-at-reducing-recidivism/1431527039942/?ur3=1.

Valentine, E. J., and Redcross, C. (2015). Transitional jobs after release from prison: effects on employment and recidivism. *IZA Journal of Labor Policy, 4*(1), 1–17. http://dx.doi.org/10.1186/s40173-015-0043-8.

Visher, C. A., and Travis, J. (2003). Transitions from prison to community: Understanding individual pathways. *Annual Review of Sociology, 29*(1), 89–113.

Visher, C., Debus, S., and Yahner, J. (2008, October). Employment after prison: A longitudinal study of releasees in three states. Retrieved March 23, 2023, from https://www.urban.org/sites/default/files/publication/32106/411778-Employment-after-Prison-A-Longitudinal-Study-of-Releasees-in-Three-States.PDF.

Visher, Debus-Sherrill, S. A., and Yahner, J. (2011). Employment after prison: A longitudinal study of former prisoners. *Justice Quarterly, 28*(5), 698–718. https://doi.org/10.1080/07418825.2010.535553.

Welsh, W. (2007). A multisite evaluation of prison-based therapeutic community drug treatment. *Criminal Justice and Behavior, 34*(11), 1481–98. https://doi.org/10.1177/0093854807307036.

Wexler, E. (2016, June 24). Prisoners to get 'second chance Pell.' *Inside Higher Ed.* https://www.insidehighered.com/news/2016/06/24/us-expands-pell-grant-program-12000-prison.

Wexler, H. K. (1995). The success of therapeutic communities for substance abusers in American prisons. *Journal of Psychoactive Drugs*, *27*(1), 57–66. https://doi.org / 10.1080/02791072.1995.10471673.

Wexler, H. K., Falkin, G. P., and Lipton, D. S. (1990). Outcome evaluation of a prison therapeutic community for substance abuse treatment. *Criminal Justice and Behavior*, *17*(1), 71–92. https://doi.org/10.1177/0093854890017001006.

Whelan, C. (2020, June 29). The importance of prison rehabilitation programs before and after release. Retrieved March 23, 2023, from https://www.iwf.org/2020/06/29/the-importance-of-prison-rehabilitation-programs-before-and-after-release/.

Winterfield, L., Coggeshall, M., Burke-Storer, M., Correa, V., and Tidd, S. (2009). The effects of postsecondary correctional education: "Final report." Urban Institute (NJ1).

Wise, C. (2020, December 31). Leaving prison without a government ID can block access to housing, jobs and help. PBS.org. https://www.pbs.org/newshour/nation/leaving-prison-without-a-government-id-can-block-access-to-housing-jobs-and-help.

World Population Review. (2023). Prison Population by State 2023. Retrieved March 24, 2023, from https://worldpopulationreview.com/state-rankings/prison-population-by-state.

Yelowitz, A., and Bollinger, C. (2019, July). targeting intensive job assistance to ex-offenders by the nature of offense. Christopher Bollinger.com. http://christopherbollinger.com/wp-content/uploads/2019/09/InmatesPaper.pdf.

About the Author

Cathy Cowling is associate professor and director of criminal justice at Campbell University. She graduated three times from Campbell University and received her PhD in criminology and criminal justice from Old Dominion University in 2011. Prior to teaching at Campbell, Dr. Cowling served as a staff attorney at Legal Aid in Fayetteville, North Carolina. She is proud mother to Beth and lives in Coats, North Carolina.